WILLIAM D. HENSLEE

D1565173

THIRD EDITION

Entertainment Careers for Lawyers

FIRST AND SECOND EDITIONS ENTITLED *ENTERTAINMENT LAW CAREERS*

Law Practice Division | Law Student Division | Forum on Entertainment and Sports Industries

Commitment to Quality: The Law Practice Division is committed to quality in our publications. Our authors are experienced practitioners in their fields. Prior to publication, the contents of all our books are rigorously reviewed by experts to ensure the highest quality product and presentation. Because we are committed to serving our readers' needs, we welcome your feedback on how we can improve future editions of this book.

Cover design by RIPE Creative, Inc.

Library of Congress Cataloging-in-Publication Data

Henslee, William D., author.
   Entertainment careers for lawyers / by William D. Henslee. -- Third edition.
      pages cm. -- (Career series / American Bar Association.)
   Previous edition had title: Entertainment law careers.
   Includes bibliographical references and index.
   ISBN 978-1-62722-232-7 (alk. paper)
   1. Entertainers--Legal status, Laws, etc.--United States. 2. Performing arts--Law and legislation--United States. 3. Law--Vocational guidance--United States. I. Henslee, William D., author. Entertainment law careers. II. American Bar Association. Law Practice Management Division, sponsoring body. III. American Bar Association. Law Student Division, sponsoring body. IV. Title.
   KF299.E57H46 2014
   344.73'099023--dc23

                                                              2013045198

Dedication

To Elizabeth, John, and James for their love and encouragement. To Frances for always believing. To Phil Damon for inspiring me to begin. And, to Doug, who will live forever in my memories.

Contents

About the Author

William D. Henslee is a Professor at Florida A&M University College of Law where he teaches Entertainment Law, Copyright Law, Trademark and Unfair Competition Law, Intellectual Property Survey, Labor Law, Legal Writing, Sports Law, Theater Law, and Travel Law. Prior to becoming a founding faculty member at FAMU, Professor Henslee taught at Pepperdine University School of Law. Professor Henslee received his Bachelor of Arts Degree in English with an emphasis in Creative Writing from the University of Hawaii. He received his Juris Doctorate from Pepperdine University School of Law. Professor Henslee received a Masters of Fine Arts Degree from the Graduate School of Theater, Film and Television at the University of California, Los Angeles.

Professor Henslee began his entertainment business career as a music manager prior to attending law school. Following law school, he formed a law firm specializing in representing music clients. Since beginning his teaching career, he has continued to consult with some clients on a limited basis. He served as the plaintiff's expert in *Brown v. Far Out Productions*. Professor Henslee continues to own a music publishing company he established in 1986. Professor Henslee worked as a certified contract advisor for the National

Football League Players Association for ten years before retiring. He was a co-producer on the independent film *Karaoke King* and a producer and writer for Michael Reardon's *Climb On* series. Professor Henslee sold his first pitch for a television sitcom while in film school. The rights have since reverted to him. Over the years, he has represented talent, athletes, independent production companies, independent record companies, and music publishing companies.

While riding with a client to a California Labor Board hearing, Professor Henslee commented that the client's new back-up singers were not really adding to the show. The client, the lead singer for a band that had had two number one singles over the years said, "Have you seen the movie *This is Spinal Tap?*" Professor Henslee responded that he makes his entertainment law students watch the film as part of his class. The client said, "That is my life. My keyboard player's girlfriend is one of the back-up singers and now she has become the manager of the band. We are doomed." He quit touring with the band shortly after that.

Acknowledgments

The Career Series is a project of the American Bar Association Law Student Division, the Law Practice Division, and many ABA volunteers who have helped to create an informative monograph series designed to give students and practitioners accurate information on the realities of practice in specialized areas of law.

Information for the monographs is gathered from research on the specialty area of practice and from personal interviews with lawyers.

In addition to the lawyers listed below who were kind enough to share their time and expertise to aid in the preparation of this monograph, the author would like to thank the lawyers who participated in the interview process but who preferred to remain anonymous. For reviewing the manuscript and offering substantive comments on the first edition, special thanks goes to Lynn Strudler, Ellen Wayne, Percy Luney, Barbara Lano, and Frances Henslee. For assistance with the second edition, I would like to thank Carol Allemeier and Eric Griffin for their comments and research. For assistance with the third edition, I would like to thank Elizabeth Henslee, Frances Henslee, and Ellen Wayne.

In addition to the anonymous lawyers who helped make all three editions an accurate reflection of the realities of entertainment practice, I would like to thank the following individuals listed in alphabetical order: Delynn Y. Axelberg, Marc S. Banco, Lain C. Baillie, Carolyn Blackwood, Guy S. Blake, Kevin C. Boyle, Elliott H. Brown, Jeff Burke, Richard Colby, Jessica Darraby, Nalinya Davis, Peter Dekom, Elizabeth Dusinberre, Martin A. Fine, Don Fendel, Nadine J. Fingert, Darren Forster, Scott Frazier, Jay A. Froberg, Stephen T. Freeman, Melissa Glousman Arbiter, Gary Greenberg, Robert Gumer, Eric Griffin, Elizabeth Henslee, Tom Henslee, Josh Hiller, Gordon Hvolka, Jonathan W. Janove, Craig S. Kamins, Leonard Korobkin, Steven Kotlowitz, Molly LaBelle, Richard Levin, Shannon Ligon, Peggy Lisberger, Steven R. Lowry, Chris Lucero, David W. Maker, Martin A. Mansfield, Jr., Andrew M. Manshul, Peter Marco, Mona Metwalli, Bill Meyer, Julee Milham, Gary Munneke, Scott Noe, Eric Norwitz, Michael A. Novak, Emmanuel E. Nunez, Jenna Piccolo, Roger L. Prillman, Patrick Rajasingam, Grace Reiner, J. Richard Ryan, Dominic Salfi, Steven G. Saltman, Jenna Sanz-Agero, Dan Satorius, Robert M. Segal, Jody Silverman, Harold Strudler, John H. Sucke, Anita Surendran, Joe ThurdeKoos, D. Thomas Triggs, Donald J. Tringali, John Ward, Glenn Weisberger, William Whitacre, Cassandra Willard, Steven Wroe, Joseph Yanny, and Christa Zofcin.

Special thanks to the following non-lawyers who contributed insights for this book: Ramza Aleem, Kenia Ashby, Glen Barclay, Hannah Buchdahl, Harold Brown, Michael Cord, Bob DiCerbo, B.B. Dickerson, Lalita Garrett, John Higgins, Bill Hill, Steve Gold, Doug Howe, Tanner Patrick Howe, Brian James, Bobby Key, Gordon Kim, Anil Kumar, Eric Lindell, Bertram MaCann, Lee Oskar, Andy Perrott, J.J. Ruscella, Shelley Saltman, Edward Sanchez, Marcus Sanchez, Howard Scott, Tom Stroup, and Fee Waybill.

Foreword

The American Bar Association's Career Series is designed to give students and beginning practitioners practical information on choosing and following career paths in the practice of law. Books in the series offer realistic, first-hand accounts of practicing law in specialized substantive areas and guidance on setting and reaching career goals.

The Career Series evolved during the ABA's 1982 Annual Meeting as a joint project of the Section of Economics of Law Practice, the Law Student Division, and the Standing Committee on Professional Utilization and Career Development. Working together, these three entities formed the Career Series Steering Committee, which is now the ABA's official clearinghouse for career-oriented publications. The members of this committee are lawyers, law students, and administrators themselves and understand the need for educated career choices. They have geared the Career Series toward meeting the needs of students and lawyers contemplating career decisions.

Since 1982, many committee members have worked to produce this series of books, and we would like to thank some of them. Gary Munneke, Theodore Orenstein, Monica Bay, Julie Moore, Joseph Cassachi, Thomas Wynn, Lynn Strudler, Carol Kanarek, Ellen

Wayne, Peggy Podell, and Percy Luney have all been instrumental in establishing, developing, and maintaining the Career Series. In addition, the committee has relied on Tim Johnson and other ABA staff.

Our committee's goal is to help lawyers secure satisfying jobs in their chosen areas of practice. To this end, the Career Series Steering Committee presents this publication to complement the Career Series.

Chapter 1
WHAT IS ENTERTAINMENT LAW?

Many non-entertainment lawyers and students picture the practice of entertainment law as a glamorous way to mix with the rich and famous while earning a huge income. It is seen as an easy road to fortune, glamorous parties, gala events, and national recognition if you can just get that first break.

Reality is quite different. Like any other specialty area of law practice, entertainment lawyers work long hours and work hard. Entertainment law specialists usually develop an expertise in one or more of the substantive areas of law that combine to form the body of entertainment law such as copyright, contracts, trademark, labor (including child labor laws), employment law, worker's compensation, tax, business organizations, antitrust, administrative law, bankruptcy, family law, immigration, or criminal law. In addition, entertainment lawyers typically focus on transactional work or litigation. Intellectual property and contracts law are often the subject matter of industry agreements. Understanding the entertainment business is the key to understanding the industry terms of art that have developed through contract forms and litigation.

It is no longer accurate to state that there is no such thing as entertainment law because entertainment law is simply the amalgamation of several disparate areas of substantive law and business. Nevertheless, it is an extremely popular area of law for students and a career target for practitioners.

What is the draw? Perhaps it is the opportunity to participate in the creation of a work that has the potential to affect the lives of people around the world for years to come. Or perhaps it is the entertainment lawyer's clients who make this unique practice area appealing. Potential clients can include those listed in the box on pages 3–5 and various other individuals and groups connected with the entertainment business.

As with any final entertainment product viewed by the general public, appearances can be deceiving. Months, and sometimes years, of behind-the-scenes work goes into the final two-hour movie, weekly television show, Broadway production, or CD. Some of that work is done by lawyers. Much of the legal work ends when the details of the project's contracts are complete. At that time, the "talent" begins work on the product that will be released to the consumer.

In addition to an overview of the substantive law areas included in entertainment law, four major entertainment genres will be discussed in this book: music, theater, film, and television. We will also take a brief look at representing artists and writers. The Internet and video games will be discussed as they provide opportunities to practice entertainment law. We will examine each area from several angles to illustrate the specific demands of a specialty practice and help sort out the pros and cons of developing a practice in entertainment law. In dispelling some of the myths surrounding an entertainment practice, many "terms of art" will be used. These terms are defined in Appendix A.

POTENTIAL CLIENTS IN AN ENTERTAINMENT LAW PRACTICE

The following list is merely a sample of potential clients for an entertainment practitioner.

Multinational Corporations

Internet Providers
Motion Picture Studios
Network and Cable Television Companies
Radio Stations
Record Companies
Music Publishing Companies
Satellite and Direct TV
Theater Groups

Corporations, Partnerships, and Other Business Entities

Production Companies
Film Financers (Foreign and Domestic)
Foreign Sales Agents
Independent Record Companies
Music Publishing Companies
Performance Rights Societies (ASCAP, BMI, and SESAC)
The Harry Fox Agency and Soundscan
Theater Groups
Video Game Companies

Unions

American Federation of Television and Recording Artists
Screen Actors Guild
Screen Extras Guild
Directors Guild of America

National Association of Broadcast Engineers and Technicians
American Federation of Musicians
The Authors Guild
Writers Guild of America

Individuals

Actors
Agents
Artists
Cartoonists
Cinematographers
Club Owners
Columnists
Comedians
Comedy Writers
Computer Graphic Artists
Critics
Directors
Film Editors
Illustrators
Individual Corporate Officers and Employees
Individual Union Members
Intellectual Property Infringers
Managers
Musicians
News Anchors and Reporters
Non-union Talent
Non-union Crew
Novelists
Photographers
Playwrights
Producers
Programmers

Screenwriters
Songwriters
Stunt Artists
Video Game Creators

Miscellaneous

Internet Providers
Merchandising Companies
Restaurants and Retail Outlets
Sports Franchises
Theme Parks
Video Game Companies

Points of Entry

If you picture the entertainment industry as a train with the potential for growth in many different areas, Figure 1.1 may be helpful to visualize the many points of entry into the entertainment business. The list is not exhaustive. It is meant to stimulate your creativity.

Television	Music	Film	Theater
News			
O&O's (Owned & Operated local stations)			
Affiliates			
Talent Agent			
Literary Agent			
Satellite Television			
Cable Television			
Production Company			
Reality Programs			
Cartoons			
Television Movies			
Adventure Sports			Talent Agent
Hockey			Literary Agent
Football		Talent Agent	Production Company
Baseball		Literary Agent	Cartoons
Basketball		Satellite Television	Movies
NASCAR		Cable Television	Advertising Agency
Golf		Production Company	Set Design Shop
Tennis		Reality Programs	Sound Stage
Boxing		Cartoons	Back Lot
Mixed Martial Arts		Pay-per-view	Lighting Equipment
Extreme Sports		Advertising Agency	Camera Equipment
Pay-per-view	Record Company	Set Design Shop	Transportation Company
Advertising Agency	Recording Studio	Sound Stage	Electrical Equipment
Set Design Shop	Terrestrial Radio	Back Lot	Craft Services
Sound Stage	Talk Radio	Lighting Equipment	Catering
Back Lot	Satellite Radio	Camera Equipment	Coaches
Lighting Equipment	Internet Radio	Transportation Company	Talent Management
Camera Equipment	Concert Hall	Electrical Equipment	Internet Management
Transportation Company	Retail Record Store	Craft Services	Web Design
Electrical Equipment	Music Publishing	Catering	Broadway venue
Craft Services	Vinyl Pressing Plant	Coaches	Off-Broadway venue
Catering	CD Pressing Plant	Talent Management	Dramaturge
Coaches	Street Team	Internet Management	Actors
Talent Management	Music Festivals	Web Design	Dancers
Internet Management	Tour Management	Writers	Singers
Web Design	Tour Transportation	Directors	Orchestra
Product placement	Booking Agent	Producers	Traveling companies
Writers	Artist Management	Line producers	Transportation
Directors	Talent	Actors	Wardrobe
Producers	Mixing Studio	Wardrobe	
Wardrobe	Producers		
	Songwriters		

Figure 1.1   Points of Entry to Entertainment Careers

Chapter 2
SUBSTANTIVE LAW AREAS

Law schools have adapted to meet the needs of students with a potential interest in entertainment law. Recently developed courses provide a background in substantive specialties needed for an entertainment practice, and they introduce students to entertainment business issues that affect legal decisions. Most law schools now have at least one course on entertainment law and business. Several law schools offer an "emphasis" or a certificate program in entertainment law and/or intellectual property. There are numerous LL.M. degrees in both intellectual property and entertainment law. Intellectual property law courses are typically included in entertainment law curricula, and entertainment law courses are typically included in intellectual property law curricula.

Since entertainment law is simply the practice of several substantive specialty areas of law in the entertainment industry, expertise in a related substantive area of law is often the best way to get that first assignment that can be developed into a practice. After all, it is the client who makes the practice of contract law or labor law or intellectual property law become entertainment law. Many industry entry-level positions and opportunities require expertise in tax, business, labor, intellectual property, or some other related area of law. This expertise is usually gained through practice after law school graduation and admission to the bar.

This chapter highlights the major areas of substantive law practiced in the entertainment industry. The following sections are offered as a cursory review of the subjects covered and are not intended to be discussions of the complexities of the individual specialty areas.

INTELLECTUAL PROPERTY

Intellectual property rights are often the subject of industry contracts. The acquisition and exploitation of those rights provide the industry with products for sale and distribution.

Expertise in copyright is a prerequisite for contract negotiations concerning music, plays, film scripts, television scripts, video game scripts, or novels. Many industry projects are considered "works for hire" so that the production company owns the individual artistic contributions of the talent, such as the writer, director, and actors, who would otherwise have rights in their individual creations.

In addition to knowledge of federal copyright law, lawyers need to be familiar with the standard industry intellectual property rights and the requirements for the assignment of those rights. Talent contracts include clauses on the rights to the creative contribution, the assignment of the intellectual property rights involved, and the royalty distributions for the exploitation of those underlying intellectual property rights.

While copyright law is a major substantive law area affecting most relationships in the entertainment industry, trademark law is an area of expertise generally required by the businesses involved in distributing and selling the products. Every network, studio, and production company has a distinctive trademark or brand, and protecting the brand is a full-time job at the major studios. While virtually all major touring acts have registered trademark names and logos, many new acts do not or cannot because of cost or lack of expertise. To protect the branded intellectual property of both the corporate businesses and individual talent—regardless of their size or longevity—a practitioner needs to be familiar with trademark law.

Patent law is generally not a requirement for an intellectual property lawyer specializing in the entertainment business. Most of the intellectual property created for entertainment purposes is protected by copyright and trademark law. However, developments in Computer Generated Images (CGI), Imax and 3-D cameras, videogame equipment, internet development, and other inventions may require patent protection. For these developments in entertainment, a patent law specialist is needed. If you have a science background and are eligible to take the patent bar, the additional credential should help your employment prospects.

CORPORATE AND BUSINESS LAW

Lawyers engaged in the practice of corporate law develop skills that are transferable and applicable in an entertainment practice. Clients' needs range from forming a business organization and preparing annual reporting to major mergers and acquisitions. While these tasks performed for a large manufacturing firm would likely be similar in the various manufacturing industries, the corporate requirements of an artist or author vary from the requirements of a producer or publisher. Large entertainment conglomerates have problems similar to those of non-entertainment industry corporations related to such issues as compliance with federal and state regulations, governance, leadership succession, tax, employment, and acquisitions.

Loan-out corporations are created by talent (including, but not limited to, actors, directors, producers, bands, and singers) to shield the individual or group from individual liability for breach of contract, or torts committed by the individual while working for the corporation. Loan-out corporations also allow the individual to plan for tax compliance, acquire health insurance, and create a retirement plan.

Main Line Pictures, Inc. v. Basinger, 1994 WL 814244, is an example of a loan-out corporation being used to protect the individual from damages for breach of contracts. In this case, Kim Basinger was sued for breach of contracts for backing out of her agreement to star in the movie *Boxing Helena*. The jury awarded Main Line Pictures $8,000,000 against Ms. Basinger and her loan-out company, Mighty Wind. The case was reversed because the jury instructions did not differentiate between Ms. Basinger and her loan-out company, making the award of damages ambiguous as to who was responsible for the damages.

Independent filmmakers will often form a limited liability corporation in order to raise money for a particular film. The limited liability company shields the producers from personal liability in the case of financial losses for any reason. Separate limited liability corporations for separate projects allow the producers to protect the profitable projects from those that do not perform as well. In effect, the limited liability corporation avoids cross-collateralization for a producer working on several independent projects.

Broadcast industry corporations often include as a member of their in-house corporate law department a communications law expert who knows how to comply with the Federal Communications Act Regulations promulgated by the Federal Communications Commission. Complex regulatory problems may require the association of outside counsel in the corporation's home state as well as in Washington, D.C.

The major entertainment conglomerates have continued to merge seeking synergy and efficiency by combining creative departments as well as the other departments necessary to run a corporation such as Human Resources.

The preceding are examples of ways corporate law experts practice in the entertainment industry. While a basic knowledge of corporate law practice can facilitate entry into the entertainment field, each corporate client in the entertainment industry has specialized needs. Familiarity with the business aspects of a particular specialty in the entertainment field combined with an understanding of the interrelationships with other businesses, unions, and individuals is essential for quality client representation.

ANTITRUST LAW

Over the years, the entertainment industry has kept many antitrust lawyers busy. Back in the 1940s, the major film studios were sued by the federal government for vertically integrating the industry. The Paramount Decrees [see *United States v. Paramount Pictures, Inc.,* 334 U.S. 131 (1948)] settled the cases. The Decrees still apply to the studios that were signatories to the settlement. The signatory studios are not allowed to own exhibition theaters while the non-signatory studios have acquired theaters as the industry has consolidated.

ASCAP and BMI were both charged with antitrust violations when they attempted to negotiate with venues and broadcast stations for performance royalties [see *Broadcast Music, Inc. v. Columbia Broadcasting Systems, Inc.,* 441 U.S. 1 (1979)]. Their activities are limited based on the outcomes of those cases. Blanket licenses for the performance of music are allowed.

Antitrust concerns were the basis for the Financial Syndication Rules that prevented network broadcasters from owning the shows they broadcast [see *In the Matter of Amendment of Part 73 of the Commission's Rules and Regulations with Respect to Competition and Responsibility in Network Television Broadcasting,* 23 F.C.C.2d 382 (1970)]. Regulations also limited the networks' ability to own local channels so as to ensure diversity in news and content coverage. The

Financial Syndication Rules have been repealed and the limits on market penetration have been relaxed.

Nevertheless, as multinational entertainment conglomerates merge to capture a greater share of the market, antitrust lawyers and lobbyists will be required to negotiate the company mergers and negotiate with the government to allow them.

TAX LAW AND GENERAL ACCOUNTING

Tax law is closely related to the corporate practice area. Again, where general corporate and/or individual tax expertise is required for an entertainment tax practice, industry clients have special tax planning and budgeting problems. Many individuals receive cash advances and some form of passive royalty income based on sales or box office grosses. Others receive large lump sum payments plus residuals each time their program or commercial is "aired." Individuals may also go for extended periods of time without a salary while living off invested money from an earlier project.

Entertainment industry businesses must keep track of huge budget expenditures and allocate income to specific projects. Each project has production and marketing costs as well as "talent" advances and royalties or residuals. Each project budget must be prepared in light of the entire company's operating budget. Budgets can be as high as $200,000,000 for a single film. Television programs can have a weekly budget of $1,000,000 or more, and recording budgets can reach $1,000,000 or more.

Record contracts may include cross-collateralization of costs, with all of the artist's income from all of the artist's work for the company included in the calculation. In some cases, the cross-collateralization may include music-publishing income. Recording artists only recoup the recording costs at their individual royalty percentage, so the record company will cover its actual expenses before the artist's recording fund is recouped by the artist. Artist royalties are only triggered after the recording fund is recouped. Hit records have to pay for all of the projects that do not appeal to the masses.

Studio accounting requires an inside knowledge of how film projects are expensed and how the costs are recouped. The definitions of *gross* and *net income* are fiercely negotiated and the sections can take pages of legalese to cover. (See Buchwald v. Paramount Pictures Corp., 1992 WL 1462910 for an example of net income litigation.) There are several levels of gross point and net point participants and each level has a complex formula for calculating the amount due under the clause. There have been a number of lawsuits challenging the accounting of a particular project.

Generally, the studio takes its distribution fee of between 15 and 50 percent of the box office gross off the top. Then the studio pays itself for the cost of the P&A (prints and ads). Then, if there is anything left, the studio's overhead is deducted; interest on the gross budget is deducted; and gross-point participants' bonuses are deducted. If the film has a first-dollar, gross-point participant, it will never generate net income. Net points are included in the contracts of writers, directors, and actors who do not have the clout to negotiate a gross-point position. Eddie Murphy commented that the net points that were being debated in *Buchwald v. Paramount Pictures Corp,* 1992 WL 1462910, were nothing but "monkey points" because according to studio accounting practices, no studio movie ever recouped its costs, so the net-point participants could expect nothing in the way of back-end participation. While there was a discussion that talent compensation would change after the *Buchwald* case, the only things that changed were the terms of art. Studios are in business to make money, so the most financially successful films have to cover the losses generated by the films that fail at the box office.

Video games, like films, hire talent for a flat fee or for an upfront fee and some percentage of back-end participation. Music is either licensed for a flat fee or for an upfront fee and some form of per-unit royalty payable after the upfront fee is recouped.

Television accounting varies from film and music because the initial fees are designed to cover the salaries and costs of producing the program. Networks now co-produce and own all or part of the programs they broadcast. Expiration of the financial syndication (Fin/Syn) laws that governed the industry for decades has facilitated the change. The network receives income from advertising and retransmission fees to cover its costs of producing the program. Recently, networks have demanded, and received, fees from satellite and cable companies for the right to carry the channel. This change in television economics now allows the broadcast networks to match the revenue streams of their rival specialty networks on cable and satellite. A television production company makes its most significant income when a show is sold into syndication. Prior to network consolidation and the repeal of the financial syndication rules, a production company typically needed one hundred episodes in order to sell the show in syndication. Now, networks will syndicate their prime time shows on a sister cable network with as few as six episodes completed. After the program is sold into syndication, the income flowing to talent comes from union negotiated residuals.

Tax lawyers and accountants are employed by both individuals and companies in the industry. A tax specialist can provide a valuable service to an industry client by bringing tax planning and budgeting expertise into every contract negotiation and project proposal. A number of high-level lawyers working in the entertainment industry have tax backgrounds and/or are Certified Public Accountants. Many law schools offer LL.M. programs in tax. The additional credentials can distinguish candidates for a particular job that includes business planning and an understanding of the legal aspects of the transactions involved. In a business where large sums of money are spent on each project, a tax background can be an invaluable asset.

LABOR LAW

The entertainment industry as a whole is one of the most unionized industries in the United States. Except for management and sales, most individuals involved in the industry belong to a union.

Industry unions are usually called guilds to avoid the negative connotations associated with unions. Guild members generally feel like they are more highly skilled than union members. Actors, actresses, "extras," directors, musicians, vocalists, set builders, writers, stunt performers, camera technicians, sound and light technicians, and transportation specialists all generally belong to an industry guild.

Guild agreements specify the terms of employment and minimum work conditions for all members. Wage agreements are generally minimums allowing individuals with special talent or skill to negotiate a higher pay scale, and if available, some form of back-end participation (gross or net points). Many industry contract clauses are nonnegotiable based on the interrelationship of talent, unions, and business and the historical development of the clause through years of union/management contract negotiation and litigation.

Several states have labor code provisions governing the procurement of employment by agents, managers, and lawyers on behalf of their clients. Understanding the local laws governing the solicitation of employment is critical when working with talent.

Labor is one of the more highly sought specialties within the industry. Many entry-level positions require a labor law background, and this type of experience has provided many lawyers with opportunities in the entertainment field.

EMPLOYMENT LAW

In-house legal departments usually have at least one lawyer who is conversant in employment law. Human resources departments provide administrative services to everyone from the janitorial staff to the CEO. Each level of employment has its own issues. In addition, as discussed above, some employees may belong to a union, and others may be exempt. By law, management-level employees may not belong to a union. In all cases, an employee's rights are governed by federal law, state law, and corporate policy that must conform to the law. In some cases, the head of the human resources department may have legal training.

California has specific laws governing individual service contracts. The "seven-year" statute generally limits a personal service contract to seven years from the commencement of service. (See De Haviland v. Warner Bros. Pictures, Inc., 67 Cal. App. 2d 225, 153 P.2d 983 (1944) for a discussion of the seven year rule.) It has been amended at the behest of the recording industry. In addition, California requires that a record company guarantee an artist a minimum income, based on the number of years of the contract, for the contract to be enforced in equity.

In addition, California requires companies that deem an individual's creative contribution to a project a "work for hire" to pay state unemployment taxes and worker's compensation tax. These California laws make the choice-of-forum clause a very important one.

The entertainment industry has been notorious for using unpaid interns, both legal and non-legal, as a way for employers to get free labor in exchange for providing work experience and contacts to the interns. These practices have recently come under scrutiny by Congress, the courts [See Glatt v. Fox Searchlight Pictures, Inc., 2013 WL 2495140 (S.D.N.Y. 2013) for a decision on the subject.] and the Internal Revenue Service. Studios, production companies, record companies, television stations, and any other entity that uses unpaid interns will have to pay close attention to changes in the law to avoid penalties and fines. An employment expert will be able to protect the company from legal action by keeping the company in compliance with changes in the law.

CRIMINAL LAW

Unfortunately, actors and musicians occasionally get in trouble with the law. It is not uncommon for a celebrity to be stopped for driving under the influence, be charged for domestic violence, or assault a particularly annoying paparazzo. The criminal prosecution of celebrities is widely reported in the media. The combination of a celebrity's public persona and the media attention given to the problem makes the lawyer's job more challenging than it would be in a similar situation involving private individuals. For lawyers who work with talent, it is important to have a basic understanding of criminal law and have a professional relationship with a criminal defense lawyer who can assist a client in trouble.

Brushes with the law are certainly not limited to athletes, actors and musicians, but those are the cases that receive the most publicity. Just as criminal legal problems can affect any member of the public, they can affect anyone associated with the entertainment business. Well-known individuals tend to hire well-known lawyers who have a reputation for dealing with high profile cases. Before establishing a private criminal defense practice, working as a prosecutor or public defender is very helpful experience.

FAMILY LAW

The need for a knowledge of family law, a specialty peripheral to entertainment law, unfortunately arises during the course of representing individuals involved in the industry. Because of the nature of the industry, entertainers and executives are often away from home for long periods, which can cause stress in any relationship. These individuals often have a relatively high net worth. A significant number of industry people have multiple marriages and divorces, which require a lawyer's expertise negotiating prenuptial and separation agreements and in handling divorce and custody issues. Once again, the fact that a client's every move may be widely reported in gossip papers and magazines can complicate the lawyer's job.

When talent is under the age of eighteen, a lawyer needs knowledge of specific state statutes governing child employment. Enforceability of the contract depends on compliance with the law. Some states require a trust be created to protect the child's income for the future. Knowledge of the state law of the child's domicile is required in order to effectively represent talent under the age of eighteen.

ESTATE PLANNING

High net worth individuals need experienced estate planners to preserve their family's wealth. Trusts are often used to protect assets and prevent children from squandering their inheritance. Is an estate planner an entertainment lawyer? It depends on how you define the term, but estate planners are essential for successful entertainment executives and entertainers.

LITIGATION

While the bulk of the legal work done in the entertainment industry is transactional, some professional relationships do deteriorate to the point where litigation is required. Litigation skills are usually coupled with a background in the substantive area being litigated.

Most entertainment corporations hire outside counsel to handle their litigation. A member of the corporate legal staff will work with outside counsel and direct the litigation for the company, but the actual litigation will be handled by an outside firm. In Los Angeles and New York, there are several prominent law firms that specialize in entertainment industry litigation.

To generalize, while many entertainment practitioners have had some litigation experience, the majority of the work involves negotiation and drafting. As one entertainment lawyer said, "For every one lawyer making a living litigating entertainment law cases, there are roughly thirty involved solely in a transactional practice."

CONTRACT NEGOTIATIONS

Contract negotiation requires a basic understanding of contracts law coupled with expertise in labor, employment, real estate, tax, trademark, and/or copyright law. In addition, an understanding of the particular entertainment industry business is critical for effective representation.

Industry experience is a major asset when involved in a contract negotiation. Knowledge of common industry practices and the terms of art are necessary to communicate effectively with opposing counsel during negotiations. The ability to translate the terms of art into "English" is important and allows the client to make the critical decisions necessary to close the deal based on a thorough understanding of the contract.

Negotiating industry contracts involves as much business acumen as it does an understanding of the relevant substantive law. Industry lawyers read the same trade papers as industry executives, and most also read the *Los Angeles Times* because it includes important business information about the entertainment industry. Business lunches and CLE programs keep industry lawyers up-to-date on the latest trends in the industry and their ramifications on the law.

When negotiating a particular deal, demonstrating a knowledge of which terms of the contract are negotiable and which terms of the contract are boilerplate (and can be negotiated depending on the power of the negotiating party) is helpful. A basic understanding of negotiable issues can be gained from reading industry form contracts, but there is no substitute for experience in contract negotiations.

BANKRUPTCY LAW

Technological innovation and the economy have forced some companies to reorganize in order to compete. Individuals have been forced to seek bankruptcy protection as the economy and the housing market have suffered during the recession. The stigma of bankruptcy has been erased by the long recession.

Individuals have used bankruptcy to avoid judgments and oppressive contracts. After losing the *Boxing Helena* case, previously discussed, Kim Basinger declared bankruptcy to avoid paying the judgment. At the time, *The New York Times* wrote an article on how the bankruptcy laws were being manipulated by Ms. Basinger to avoid her judgment. The paper showed a picture of Ms. Basinger's town in Georgia and exposed the fact that she was paying $7,500 per month for pet care. Ultimately, the court did not allow Ms. Basinger to avoid the judgment and she had to sell her town to pay the judgment.

Recording artists have attempted to use bankruptcy as a way to escape onerous contract terms. While the courts have scrutinized the good faith of the petitioner, the court did allow Toni Braxton, Run-DMC, and TLC to avoid their label contracts, allowing them to negotiate more favorable terms for future recordings.

IMMIGRATION LAW

Immigration law is a specialty area that has complicated industry projects involving foreign citizens working in this country. The Immigration and Naturalization Service is reluctant to grant entrance into the United States to an individual who is going to take a job away from an American citizen. The applicant must demonstrate unique expertise or talent in order to be granted a work visa to enter the United States for a project.

Similarly, American citizens traveling to foreign countries to work on a project may encounter difficulties abroad. For these reasons, an experienced entertainment lawyer will consult with an immigration law expert when a project involves foreign citizens working in the United States or U.S. citizens working in other countries.

CONCLUSION

While the areas of law discussed here are not the only substantive areas an entertainment lawyer will encounter, they are some of the main areas of concentration required for adequate client representation. Expertise and experience in any one of these areas may lead to a career in entertainment law.

The following chapters on music, theater, film, and television include a brief discussion of how the substantive law is integrated into the media practice areas. Personal vignettes from practitioners reveal the backgrounds, work experience, and advice on how to break into the business in each section. The vignettes are anonymous, but they are real-life stories as revealed by responses to a questionnaire. Follow-up interviews were conducted to collect accurate information about the individual profiled and his or her practice.

Lawyers practice in a variety of settings within each media concentration area. The major practice setting opportunities will be covered in each chapter.

Chapter 3

Music is a very complex practice area. It requires a practitioner to understand the business aspects of the industry as well as copyright, trademarks/service marks, labor, tax, contract negotiations, psychology, and sociology. A relationship with a good criminal lawyer is often helpful, too. State law governing the industry and the relationship of the parties varies by jurisdiction, so it behooves any lawyer to be informed about the local laws and industry customs governing the contract.

Individual clients tend to be extremely talented people with large egos. They include record company executives, artists (vocalists and musicians), producers, managers, talent agents, and investment counselors/business managers. A Los Angeles lawyer who has worked with some of the biggest bands since the 1960s said, "When God gave musicians talent, He took something away. Your job as a lawyer is to find out what is missing and provide that for your client. Usually, it is common sense."

With the Internet, and particularly YouTube, anyone can be a recording artist. The cost of recording equipment has fallen to levels that allow anyone with a little determination to record a single. Video cameras, included on computers and phones, are no longer cost prohibitive allowing anyone to become a video "star." iTunes allows artists to sell their music to the public without the benefit of a label, making their music accessible to the masses. There are no longer any significant barriers to entry in the music business. That being said, a record label is still the best way for an artist to move from an Internet sensation to a global superstar. The label provides the artist with financing, marketing, and distribution on a scale that has not been duplicated by Internet-only stars.

Music is a personality business where many attempt to compose and sing a hit song, but only a few realize that goal. While those who are successful can afford to pay legal fees, the vast majority of talented people working in the music business will never get the break they need to succeed financially. This larger group of struggling artists and producers also need legal representation, however, to protect their talents and efforts from those who might take advantage of them.

FIRMS & ENTERTAINMENT LAW

The majority of lawyers who practice law in the music business do so as members of a law firm. Firms of all sizes in New York, Los Angeles, and Nashville are usually retained by record companies to handle legal business that their in-house legal staff cannot or does not want to handle. While virtually all major record companies use in-house counsel exclusively for signing artists and making standard deals, record companies usually retain outside counsel for corporate, tax, and litigation problems. Firms are also retained to handle mergers and complex affiliation deals.

Several of the largest law firms in the country have entertainment divisions, and in media centers, entertainment boutique firms of all sizes service entertainment industry clients exclusively. Almost every city in the United States has one or more law firms specializing in entertainment law, and based on the city, the firm may or may not offer other substantive law services and litigation. Because the barriers for entry into the music business are so low, every town has a need for an entertainment lawyer specializing in the music business.

Individuals who have achieved star status often retain "name lawyers" (well-know lawyers who are stars in their own right) for their legal needs. Prominent entertainment lawyers are in demand by clients who believe certain lawyers can improve their status in the industry. Since music is a business based on talent and relationships, lawyers with a roster of talented clients develop relationships with the record company executives who give deference to a new act arriving at the label through that lawyer. Famous clients give a lawyer industry clout, which benefits the lawyer's other clients. Some lawyers now perform the function of outside A&R (Artist and Repertoire) executives for the labels by prescreening acts.

Lawyers in smaller law firms and solo practitioners often choose that setting so they have the freedom and opportunity to practice entertainment law exclusively. The reality of the situation is, however, that unless the lawyer has a major fee-producing client, the practice must expand beyond the entertainment field to pay the bills. A labor, tax, or corporate practice that allows a lawyer to develop expertise in the chosen specialty as well as the entertainment industry will usually help the lawyer attract industry clients who require assistance in one of the lawyer's specialty areas.

To stimulate income, some lawyers expand into the areas of "artist management" and booking. These situations can create a conflict of interest for the lawyer. You may want to ask for an ethical opinion from your state bar before you decide to assume a non-legal role. A lawyer acting as a manager or booking agent may find himself or herself in conflict during contract negotiations with an artist.

California, Florida, New York, and Tennessee, as well as several other states, regulate "talent agents" who book employment for touring groups. Before a lawyer agrees to find work for an entertainment client, he or she must examine the law governing solicitation of work for clients in each state the client seeks employment. The penalties for violating the law can be severe. Previously, the penalty for illegal booking was disgorgement of all of the income ever earned by the booker from the artist. As a result of a change in the law, now the booker only has to return all of the income earned from the artist in the last year.

PERCENTAGE FEES

An artist should always have separate counsel when negotiating with a lawyer for any services where the lawyer will be paid a percentage of the artist's industry income. Failure to advise a client of the need for separate counsel for the purposes of negotiating an employment contract is unethical.

In addition, percentage fee agreements are only profitable if the artist is working steadily. The income generated is usually not commensurate with the time required to handle the artist and the arrangements unless the artist is fairly successful. One way to develop a music law/business practice is to work with unknown acts for a percentage. If the act secures a record deal, a percentage of the group's success will be worth the gamble. If the act does not realize commercial success, the lawyer will have gained an education in the music business and provided needed legal services to a group or individual who could not have otherwise afforded legal representation. An artist's success can be a boon to a lawyer, manager, or booking agent working for a percentage. At some point in the artist's career, the income from the percentage may exceed the amount of time spent working with the client. Until that time, be prepared to perform a number of uncompensated hours working for your clients as they establish their career.

For lawyers who want to enter this field, the opportunity to represent someone needing legal services may seem like an entrée into the industry. However, working for a percentage is a decision that should be made with a thorough understanding of the ethical considerations and the risks involved. Be sure to consult local rules of professional responsibility for guidance on working for a percentage of an artist's income. The relationship may appear to make you a partner in the artist's enterprise depending on the scope of the activities included in the income equation. On the other hand, the arrangement could be beneficial to both parties as long as no ethical rules have been violated. Particular care should be exercised in the writing of such an agreement to guarantee it is in compliance with state contract law.

MAKING A LIVING

Entertainment law practice in many law firms is similar to practice in any other substantive specialty area in that billable hours must be generated from a number of sources to maintain the lawyer's status in the firm. Generating fees in the music business depends on the needs of the client and his or her ability to pay. While record companies, major stars, producers, managers, artists, and publishing companies can usually pay their bills, new artists and companies have difficulty making ends meet and may not pay regularly.

Lawyers who are not established or who do not have some tremendous contacts cannot expect to attract any major clients for several years of practice. Depending on the particular client, an hourly fee arrangement may be more beneficial to the client than a percentage fee relationship. Sometimes hard decisions must be made because a nonpaying client, no matter how talented that person is, will divert time and attention from those who help pay the bills.

The following personal profiles illustrate the lifestyle and workload of music lawyers practicing in law firms. The profile information is based on responses from practitioners as edited by the author. The names of lawyers and their clients have been changed.

Profile of an Entertainment Lawyer in a Medium-Size Firm

John has worked as an entertainment lawyer in a mid-sized Los Angeles firm. He went to a major law school on the East Coast, concentrating on tax and business law courses and did extra work in tax law as it relates to athletes and entertainers. During the summer between his second and third years, John clerked at the firm that hired him after graduation.

The majority of John's work was confined to California, where he is admitted to the bar. The bulk of his time was spent on the phone in his Beverly Hills office. He occasionally traveled to New York on business.

John's firm has an eight-member entertainment department and each lawyer is also responsible for clients outside the entertainment industry. John spent about 50 percent of his time on pure entertainment practice, 30 percent of his time on entertainment-related corporate matters (mergers, acquisitions, and business formations), and 20 percent of his time on unrelated corporate clients. Like all lawyers at the firm, John was expected to work long hours and produce quality work. He arrived at the office between 8:30 a.m. and 10:00 a.m. but stayed until 7:00 p.m., and many times much later. A telephone headset, similar to those worn by telephone operators, enabled him to spend the majority of his time talking to clients, agents, business managers, and other lawyers. Time off the phone was usually spent dictating letters, memos, and contracts. Typically, he handled about thirty separate matters each day.

Because his background is in tax planning, John's work at the firm involved ensuring that his clients' deals were structured to best take advantage of current tax laws. His entertainment clients have included recording artists, actors, writers, directors, record companies, and record distributors, as well as a major merchandising firm, television and motion picture producers, production companies, and motion picture studios. The clients all toil long hours and they expected John to produce quality legal work. John's clients wanted objective, sound legal advice for their fees, not a friend with whom to party.

His clients' names were recognizable and "it is exciting to hear or watch the final product of your efforts," according to John, but beyond that, he believes his work was "no more glamorous than any other lawyer's. We all worked hard and were compensated well for our efforts."

As an example of a complex deal, John cites his work on the acquisition of a small independent jazz label by a large industry conglomerate. This extremely complicated transaction involved a number of lawyers working on both sides of the acquisition. John represented the jazz label and spent several months negotiating the terms of the overall label agreement, which included royalty rates, recording advances, approvals and controls, the working agreements between the corporation and the label, the employment agreements for the key employees of the jazz label, and a buy-back provision in the event the major label did not want to continue working with the key employees. The jazz label was not dismantled, so there was no problem with the assignability of contracts currently carried in the label's catalog. Most of the label's acts were pleased with the association because a major label would now be backing their products. The acquiring company must have been pleased as well as they hired John's firm to serve as outside counsel for its overload work following the transaction.

One complicating and time-consuming factor arose when the independent label, through John, began negotiations to sign a new artist. When the merger appeared certain to be completed, the original sixty-four-page contract submitted to the artist had to be withdrawn and a second forty-page draft contract from the major label had to be submitted for the artist's approval. Because John and the subsidiary had never worked with the major label's legal department before, the contract had to be negotiated with both companies' legal departments for compliance with company standards and with the artist's lawyer. After months of delay, the artist was signed to the label.

Recently, John left the firm to become in-house counsel for a non-entertainment business client of the firm. The move allowed John to stabilize his hours and more closely control his workload. The transition has also allowed John to spend more time with his family and, he feels, it has improved his quality of life.

RECORD COMPANIES

Record companies hire lawyers to work in their business affairs departments and their legal departments. The role of the business affairs executives is to negotiate deals with recording artists. The legal department turns the negotiated deal into a long form contract. Some "labels" merge their business affairs and legal departments.

Business affairs executives fill a hybrid position that requires them to understand business, law, and creative issues. While business affairs executives are considered creative executives and may not be trained lawyers, the trend in the industry is to fill these positions with lawyers because they are the people who normally negotiate artist contracts and other creative agreements. Once a contract has been negotiated, it is sent to the legal department so the documents that memorialize the deal can be prepared. Business affairs executives propose creative contractual relationships that the legal department must turn into a representative document that both parties are willing to sign. For this reason, the legal department handles business-planning issues and creates the documents that are required for the various contractual relationships necessary to record, manufacture, and distribute an artist's product around the world. Knowledge of international copyright laws and an extensive background in both music and merchandise licensing is required to ensure the company realizes the maximum amount of income from its products.

Some of the larger labels have individuals or departments that specialize in international copyright, domestic copyright, union and guild agreements, property acquisition, and merchandising. These specialties within each area of entertainment law are usually learned through practice either at the label or at a law firm supplying this expertise to the smaller labels. Lawyers in the legal department handle the general legal problems the company encounters each day. Litigation and matters that are outside the department's expertise are farmed out to retained legal counsel as are any matters that in-house counsel are too busy to handle. In-house counsel in the music industry are no different than other in-house corporate lawyers in that respect. Like most lawyers who work as in-house corporate counselors, salaries are not as high as those of lawyers who work in law firms. Similarly, the hours are not as long as their colleagues in law firms, and working hours rarely extend to Saturdays or Sundays.

For in-house counsel, the client is the company. The artists and their managers and lawyers are initially the adversaries until an agreement is signed. After the initial signing, the in-house lawyers and business affairs executives do not work directly with the artist, but through the artist's manager, booking agent, and/or lawyer.

ROLES OF RECORD COMPANY STAFF MEMBERS

Artist and Repertoire (A&R) people are the record company employees who listen to the thousands of unsolicited tapes the record company receives from aspiring artists. Their job includes visiting local clubs in search of talent and material for their label's groups. These departments are staffed with the creative people who find and develop talent and bring them to the label. An A&R executive is the artist's inside contact at the record label.

There is an unwritten rule in the record business that states, "A&R people don't negotiate the deals and lawyers don't choose and develop the talent." Lawyers practice law and offer business advice; they do not make the companies' creative decisions. So while an A&R executive may work with lawyers or even have a law degree, the executive's job is to focus on the creative potential of a group or individual artist.

The relationship between the A&R executive and the talent is a symbiotic relationship; the talent needs the A&R person to push for good budgets, high profile marketing campaigns, good release dates, airplay, and tour support. The A&R executive needs the talent to be a commercial success in order to retain his or her position with the company. Since the company spends large sums of money based on the recommendations of the A&R executive, the A&R executive needs the talent to succeed so that the company receives a nice return on its investment. Some recording companies have an artist relations department to work with creative talent. If the label has both A&R executives and artist-relations executives, the two will work together inside the label on behalf of the talent.

Artist-relations people are assigned to shepherd the signed group through the label's bureaucracy and serve as a friend on the inside, so that marginally profitable artists do not get lost in the internal label machinery. They work with the artist's manager and booking agent to coordinate the artist's image, album and live show material, tour dates and locations, and publicity, and they ensure that the label continues to push the artist in its overall marketing plan. At some labels, the A&R people and the artist-relations people are the same. A law degree is not required or necessarily helpful in either job.

Production and distribution departments of a record company take an artist's submitted master and turn it into records and compact discs (CDs). Most labels release their artists' material online through the label's online store and iTunes as well as on CD and vinyl. The limited CD and vinyl releases have simplified the manufacturing and shipping process. Production includes designing and printing labels and jackets, inserting the record or CD into the package, and shrink-wrapping and boxing. Then the recordings are shipped to radio stations and record stores. Both shipping and returns of unsold or defective units must also be tracked by the production and distribution departments.

All labels have accounting departments to handle internal business operations as well as administer the royalty accounting that each artist's product requires. While the record company receives its income from the sale of the talent's recordings at a wholesale rate, the record company normally recoups all of the advanced recording costs from the artist at the artist's applicable royalty rate. The artist will not receive additional income from the product until all of the advances and recording costs have been recouped. Albums with high advance recording costs and low volume sales will never pay the artist a royalty. For the artist's sake, the royalty calculations require a close accounting of both sales and returns.

SoundExchange was created to collect performance royalties for record labels and the performers of the music on digital radio and the Internet. Prior to passage of the Digital Performance Right in Sound Recording Act in 1995, record companies and performers did not receive a royalty when their music was played. Songwriters and music publishers received a royalty for the performance of their musical composition, but the sound recording performers and the record companies did not. Now that the record companies have an additional revenue stream from the performance of their sound recordings, they need an accountant to track and audit the royalties.

The hierarchy of a record company is similar to any business with managers and vice presidents in charge of special areas of the company's business and a president responsible for overall label profitability. Many of the non-legal executive positions are filled by former practicing lawyers.

ARTIST REPRESENTATION

A lawyer interested in artist representation may choose a number of career paths. All major talent—artists, producers, actors, and many up-and-coming stars—have a lawyer. Attracting a known and competent industry lawyer can do as much for an artist's career as signing with the right management.

The majority of the music lawyers in the United States are located in New York, Los Angeles, and Nashville. Just as it is often important for an aspiring artist to move to one of these cities, a lawyer seeking to be an industry "heavyweight" also needs to relocate to one of these major industry meccas.

This is not to say that lawyers cannot successfully practice entertainment law in other cities across the country; there are a number of well-respected entertainment lawyers in cities outside Los Angeles, New York, and Nashville. Atlanta, Austin, Boston, Chicago, Miami, Minneapolis, Orlando, San Francisco, and Washington, DC, have significant populations of music lawyers. However, lawyers with enough industry clout that they are able to generate label interest in an artist or project based on their reputation tend to be clustered in the major media centers.

Many lawyers representing name talent work in medium- to large-sized law firms. These lawyers normally bill their clients on an hourly basis as they would bill any other individual or corporate client. In addition to an hourly rate, some lawyers negotiate bonus payments to be paid upon successful completion of a project or transaction.

Other lawyers enter into contingency fee arrangements where they take a percentage, between 3 and 15 percent, of the artist's gross income, and 5 percent of the artist's gross income is fairly common. These deals are more appealing to artists who are not yet established and cannot pay the $125 to $1,000 per hour that entertainment lawyers charge for their services.

Lawyers working in law firms report the same problems encountered as their colleagues practicing in the firm's other specialty departments. Long hours with a minimum billable hour requirement are common for a lawyer to maintain a favored status. Large law firms have experienced problems with retaining their good entertainment lawyers. Several major entertainment firms have either broken up or experienced mass defections by their entertainment lawyers. The breakaway lawyers normally feel that they can make a comfortable living outside the firm by retaining "their" clients and by attracting new clients from their current client's referrals.

Clients hire lawyers, not necessarily their law firms. The industry is quite familial, and word-of-mouth recommendations based on reputation are the key to attracting new clients.

A great number of solo and small firm practitioners also represent talent. The smaller firm environment gives the lawyer the flexibility to dedicate the unusual hours that artists demand. Often these hours are not billable. Again, fee arrangements vary with each individual situation depending upon the talent's needs, ability to pay, and the industry clout of both the lawyer and the artist. There are no set rules.

Lawyers representing talent can become involved in all aspects of the person's business and personal life. The lawyer normally handles the individual's contract negotiations with his or her manager, booking agent, record label, business manager, publishing company, producer, and the products merchandising company. The lawyer also may work on miscellaneous legal problems such as divorce, traffic problems, or any other situation where the artist should use a lawyer's services.

The following vignettes illustrate what representing a recording artist involves.

Two New Lawyers Launch a Specialty Firm

Al and Ben, two recent law graduates who had met in law school, decided to start their own firm specializing in personal and business management. Their firm attracted quite a bit of interest after receiving publicity in a local music magazine, but met with limited success and was eventually dissolved. Al is a solo practitioner in entertainment law specializing in the music industry in Los Angeles. He is not one of the industry "heavies," but his phone calls to record companies and their lawyers are eventually returned.

Prior to law school Al was a fairly successful artist manager, but made only a meager income by handling local bands. His work on that level exposed him to group management, booking, song writing, music publishing, promotions, and bookkeeping. To enhance his business background, Al enrolled in a graduate management program, but dropped out of the MBA program short of graduation to attend law school.

During law school, Al clerked with a major television network in the labor relations department and actively participated in his school's entertainment law society and the ABA Law Student Division. When Al graduated from law school, he opened a firm with Ben, a fellow law school graduate who was also a CPA. Ben had a similar background in band management and had worked in the accounting department of a Los Angeles–based cable television company.

Al and Ben hoped to establish a firm based on personal and business management, but each meeting with well-known athletes and entertainers produced a similar result. The established star was flattered by their interest, but was not willing to leave his or her current situation for an innovative but untried opportunity. After several months of refusing non-entertainment-related work and supporting a heavy negative cash flow, the lawyers decided to take part-time jobs to supplement their personal incomes. That was the beginning of the end for the firm.

The firm did attract interest from numerous local groups seeking a lawyer or "management" in order to improve the group's image in the industry. Generally speaking, a band cannot afford management or a lawyer until they are almost ready for a record deal. Most established managers will not work with unsigned groups. Most lawyers will not work with clients who cannot pay for legal services. The firm did take on two bands that received major label interest, but both bands broke up over internal personality conflicts.

The firm was written up in a local music magazine as one of the top music management firms in Los Angeles. The article caused every unsigned band in Los Angeles and several unsigned bands from other areas to send the firm a tape of their music. The notoriety did not attract any clients who could pay for the firm's services. Al and Ben dissolved the firm to pursue other work to pay the bills and to avoid receiving the ten to forty unsolicited tapes per week.

Al decided to maintain his entertainment practice while teaching bar review to support his family. Through a family connection, he attracted a jazz artist who was being approached by several labels after the release of her first album on an independent label. This was the break Al needed to elevate his practice to a respectable level in the industry.

He negotiated her major label contract, which took several hours each day over a period of weeks because of internal changes at the label. After the recording contract was completed, he prepared and negotiated the producer's contract (the artist usually hires the producer) and then reviewed and submitted the production budget. He copyrighted the artist's songs and negotiated the deal with her publishing company as well as reviewed the record label copy to ensure accurate credits.

After the album was released, Al searched for a professional manager and negotiated her contract with him. Al is still her personal advisor, business manager, and lawyer. He works closely with both the artist and her manager to ensure that both are working together to maximize her exposure and income.

He spends a couple of hours each day on the phone to the artist, manager, label's lawyer, and other necessary contacts on her behalf. Al has maintained his teaching to ensure a steady income.

Since Al began work with this major artist, he has attracted other established artists and songwriters. He is required to be very selective in choosing clients given his time limitations. He has expanded his practice to represent a songwriter, a producer, a publishing company, and a small record company.

Al's practice illustrates how much client contact one can have when representing a recording artist. During the month that the jazz artist was recording her album for the major label, Al would get phone calls at 2:00 a.m. and 3:00 a.m. to settle disputes between the producer and the artist. Because of his intervention, no dispute caused a recording session to be canceled. Prior to these calls, she would only call during reasonable working hours, unlike one of his previous, very talented clients who would call every time he had an idea, no matter what time of the day or night it was. Al reports that his wife got tired of that practice shortly after it began. Still, Al believes that his entertainment practice may not be the most successful practice in the industry, but it has been one of the more interesting practices.

"If you like late nights at the clubs and early mornings in the office (because the artists want you to be with them when they perform and in the office in the morning taking care of business) and collect phone calls at all hours of the day or night from wherever the artist happens to be, then go for it," Al says. "It is as physically demanding as it is mentally demanding." Al also says that he does not party with his clients. "They want their lawyer to be straight, not a party animal," he explains. "An artist never has trouble finding people to party with, so don't get into the work for the parties. You may have fun with your clients, but they won't trust you in a pinch if they have seen you at your worst or wildest."

Ben joined a corporate law firm where he used his CPA's knowledge as a way to pay for an office. The firm served as outside counsel for a major manufacturing corporation. Ben became a partner in the firm as the practice expanded. He practiced general business law, which included tax planning and bankruptcy.

A former classmate of Ben's was leaving his position as in-house counsel for a major studio and recommended Ben for the position in the television legal department. Even though the studio received over 250 applications, Ben was hired after several interviews because of his background in bankruptcy. His primary function was to collect money from television stations that had licensed his studio's television programs but did not pay for the programs. Ben was very successful at collecting money from the local television stations and earned a promotion.

As a vice-president, Ben expanded the scope of his duties to include intellectual property acquisitions. Ben and his boss merged the legal and business affairs departments to give them more input on the acquisitions of properties. As the economy improved and the local television stations once again became able to pay for their programming, Ben has had been able to evolve his practice to include all aspects of television property acquisition and distribution. Ben was in a highly visible position at one of the six major studios. Ben survived the downsizing that occurred since the acquisition of his company.

In his position, he frequently received calls from headhunters. Ben accepted a position as Chief Financial Officer at an independent studio. He stayed there for a few years until he accepted a position as president of an independent studio. He enjoys his ability to raise money for film projects he believes in and shepherd them from idea to completed film.

A New York Solo Act

Joan is a solo practitioner in New York City. She has a practice dedicated to entertainment, litigation, contract negotiation, copyright, and family law. Her entertainment clients include recording artists, record companies, record producers, and small businesses. Joan opened her own office after three years of work as a partner in the small entertainment law firm she joined after graduating from law school.

While a law student, she attended several Practicing Law Institute (PLI) seminars on entertainment law, and a copyright seminar by Professor David Nimmer, who wrote the leading industry treatise on the subject. Today, Joan herself is an author and currently participates in industry seminars as a speaker.

A typical day includes a brief review of the trade publications followed by phone calls to clients. In addition, each day Joan prepares and reviews documents that have evolved from her years of practice.

Joan tries to have lunch with clients or other lawyers to stay informed about industry developments. These contacts help her attract new clients through referrals as well as stay abreast of industry happenings. "Membership in either the New York or California bar is essential for an entertainment lawyer," according to Joan.

She loves her work, but finds that she works twelve-hour days with little time off. She has to put in the hours to keep up with her clients' demands. Most of her work is confined to New York, but she travels to Los Angeles and Nashville for some clients.

"Expanding technology will define the future trends in the industry," says Joan. "Right now the supply of entertainment lawyers far exceeds the demand. To break in requires expertise in a related field or tremendous contacts."

Profile of a Small Firm Lawyer

Cassandra began her entertainment law career in the corporate legal department at Planet Hollywood. After leaving Planet Hollywood, she worked at a boutique firm specializing in technology. She became proficient at licensing, merchandising, and the business and intellectual property issues involved. She started her own firm where she specializes in intellectual property and entertainment law. As she got busier, she took a partner to help her service her existing clients and attract new ones. She has worked with music festivals, graphic artists, venues, artists, actors, performers, independent filmmakers, special effects and make-up artists, promotion companies, labels, managers, and DJs. She has a transactional practice specializing in contract negotiation. In addition to her practice, Cassandra teaches Advanced Entertainment Law at Full Sail University in the Entertainment Business Masters Program. She has taught a number of entertainment and business-related courses at schools in the area.

Cassandra is active in the Florida Bar. She recently served as Chair of the Entertainment, Art & Sports Law Section of the Florida Bar. She recommends participating in the specialty bar sections and attending CLEs to network with potential employers.

Profile of a General Practitioner

Julee started her own firm right out of law school. She paid the bills by working with corporate clients for whom she had clerked during law school. The clients retained her when she passed the Florida bar, which afforded her the freedom to develop her practice independently. Her clients provided her with significant litigation experience. While her clients were not in the entertainment industry, they did have contractual issues and intellectual property problems that provided a great background for her entertainment practice.

To develop her entertainment law practice, Julee also passed the California and New York bars. She has an interesting practice that includes sitting on the bench in her judicial district eight days a month as a hearing officer. Other than the days she is scheduled for court, she has a very flexible schedule that allows her to represent clients, mediate, speak on entertainment and intellectual property issues, and work with a New York bar committee on microfinance. As an example of her schedule, one week she "talked to a promoter with a no-show artist, a copyright owner needing to license content for computerization, a composer trying to retrieve old musical works from a publisher, a manager considering a joint venture with a label, a singer/songwriter exploring termination of copyright licenses to successful songs, a filmmaker beginning a children's programming project, and a few clients coming up on trademark deadlines." She loves the variety of work that her practice generates. Her practice creates concerns with conflicts of interest and unique clients inherent throughout the entertainment industry. The most challenging part of her practice "involves contending with the parents, children, managers, agents, vocal teachers, best friends, and others who contact [her] instead of the client." Many clients "choose not to accept the strict boundaries of lawyer-client privilege."

Julee did not take an entertainment law class in law school. She recommends business law, contracts, and intellectual property classes to students. In addition, she says, "If you want to practice in radio or television, take administrative law to learn about agencies like the FCC and FTC. If you want to do film, learn about entities, unions, and securities regulations. If you are interested in first amendment issues, take media law-related classes (and note that most areas of entertainment practice require some grasp of free speech). If you enjoy the fine arts, study about non-profits, endowments, and grantwriting. Be cognizant that you will have the triple duty of knowing the industry, technology, and the law.

"Begin networking early. Check out common interest groups on www.linkedin.com. Become familiar with the Lexis entertainment industry contracts books, *Nimmer on Copyright*, and entertainment law journals and law reviews. Consider interning or volunteering at a trade organization in the area in which you are interested. Explore which industry players sponsor writing competitions and have internships. . .Subscribe to trade rags. Immerse yourself in the local entertainment or arts scene of your interest to be sure you are interested in the subculture."

Julee recommends litigation practice to learn about what happens to the contracts you draft if they don't clearly address the rights and responsibilities of both parties. "Think broadly, such as the hospital-ity, travel, and amusement industries. . . . Also, if it's the type of client you're interested in rather than the type of work, you may find your specialty is to be the divorce lawyer to entertainers, the immi-gration lawyer to entertainers, the criminal lawyer to entertainers, the tax lawyer to the entertainers, and the like. If it's the industry itself you're crazy about, you may find yourself becoming a business person within it. That could be as an executive within a company or as an owner of one, at which time there becomes a number of eth-ical issues." Whatever you do, do something you enjoy.

PERSONAL AND BUSINESS MANAGERS

A lawyer may choose not to practice law but to become a personal or business manager. Both jobs require distinct skills and tempera-ments. Information on other industry non-legal careers is in Chapter 9.

Personal managers are on call twenty-four hours a day working with the artist to develop his or her talent, style, image, and career. Good personal managers, the ones with industry clout, can make or break an act. The right words to the right people can stimulate label interest and a record deal.

Managers with that type of clout in the industry rarely take an unsigned act. Working with unsigned artists is left to the aspiring managers who hope to discover a band and rise to the top along with the act. Managing undiscovered talent is often an expensive proposition both in actual dollars and in time. It can be frustrating, but it is the career path that most big-time managers followed. Some labels will strongly request an act they are about to sign to leave their current manager for a manager with whom the label is familiar. The label's justification for the management change is based on the fact that the label is going to spend a lot of money on an album and marketing and the label wants to be confident in the manager's ability to properly develop the artist. Giving money to a new group with an untested manager is a terrifying proposition for most label executives. If the artist is loyal, the manager may survive as the manager. If the label will not agree to allow the artist to try an untested manager, the label will likely agree to allow the new manager to serve as a co-manager.

Personal management includes material selection, interview preparation, appointment making, hairstyle and make-up consultation, wardrobe and choreography selection, and even chauffeuring. In addition to the personal attention the artist expects, the artist will insist that the manager spend most of his or her time arranging shows with the booking agent, contacting the labels for a deal if the act is unsigned, or contacting the promotions department to coordinate promotions. If the act is signed, the manager must search for a producer and new material and keep tabs on all of the other people who work for the artist to ensure that they are doing their jobs.

An artist who can generate income consistently usually has a business manager to handle money and investments, as well as a personal manager. Because an artist is often on the road and unable to conduct personal business, a business manager may be in charge of handling the artist's checkbooks and credit cards to ensure that bills are paid.

Booking agents schedule and arrange personal appearances for acts and work with the personal manager and label to generate maximum exposure for each appearance. As mentioned above, many states have laws regulating agents. Check your state statutes for regulations concerning agents. While a legal education would be helpful for a personal or business manager, it is not as important as salesmanship, interpersonal skills, and personal contacts.

From Comic to Personal Manager

After graduating from college, Ray toured the U.S. as a stand-up comic. His experiences on the road taught him that he and the others needed someone who was competent to help them. While performing, he met many people who were willing to take a percentage of his income for unspecified services, but he was not impressed with the quality of representation available to him and others at his level. With encouragement from his parents, Ray attended law school to evolve his career from performer to manager.

Ray attended a West Coast law school to be close to the Los Angeles area comedy clubs so that he could supplement his income. While living in a guest house of a 60s folk singer during his first year at law school, Ray met another comic who was looking for a personal assistant. She hired Ray, and he worked as her personal assistant, making her appointments and serving as her personal valet, during his second and third years of law school. Toward the end of Ray's third year of law school, he helped the client find a caring booking agent and, after passing the bar exam, Ray evolved from personal assistant to personal manager.

His first client gave Ray industry clout and he began attracting other clients. Today, Ray works with comics who aspire to be actors and musicians. To facilitate the growth of his business, Ray partnered with a former booking agent who had worked for one of the big three agencies in Los Angeles.

Ray still works closely with his first high profile client on many projects, screening offers, and actively seeking new opportunities for her. When she got her own cable talk show, Ray became executive producer for the show. He travels extensively with his client and is on call twenty-four hours a day. Although Ray has no time for a personal life outside his job, he loves his work. He is now involved with every decision his client makes, from what to wear to which shows to accept, and how much she will get paid. It is fast-paced work that is all consuming, but Ray says he will continue to dedicate his life to furthering others' careers as long as he has clients who are willing to pay for his services.

From Professional Athlete to Personal Manager

Scott was a professional personal watercraft racer during and after college. As he began reaching the end of his career, he decided to go to law school in Northern California. He continued to race and give lessons while he studied. While in law school, he took both Sports Law and Entertainment Law. He got to know the professor and expressed his desire to have a legal career in sports and/or entertainment.

After graduating and passing the California Bar, Scott asked his professor for help in getting into entertainment or sports. His professor worked with a band that had had several hits and gold records in the 1970s and 1980s was looking for management. They were working on a comeback plan and needed a manager. The professor suggested that they consider Scott. He had to think about whether he wanted a non-legal position, but he decided to take the talk with the band. The professor arranged a meeting between Scott and the leaders of the band. After the professor convinced the band members that they could trust Scott, they hired him as their manager.

Scott has served as the personal, business, and road manager for the band. He has traveled all over the United States, Europe, and Japan with the band. Scott negotiates the contracts for the band in conjunction with their booking agent. While Scott and his professor are still close friends, Scott and the band have a love/hate relationship. They hire and fire him, or he quits, on a regular basis. The members of the band get along on stage, but they do not hang out between shows. They also have a love/hate relationship with each other. Their history of litigation goes back to 1970, and the band breaks up between gigs.

Scott found a steady job that allows him to travel with the band when necessary. He is able to telecommute for his new job if he is on the road. He works in the office when he is in town. The steady job reduces the stress of an unsteady income from the band.

MUSIC PUBLISHING

Music publishing companies exist to promote an artist's or song-writer's compositions, negotiate the royalty rates for specific uses, and collect and distribute the royalties to the individual songwriter.

Large music publishers have in-house lawyers who prepare and review their contracts. Most major record labels also operate an in-house publishing company for their artists. The majority of independent publishers hire outside counsel only when they have a special need. Since most publishing agreements follow standard forms available to songwriters through various songwriting societies, songwriters feel like there is little need for a lawyer in a standard deal. In the minds of most songwriters and publishers, a lawyer is an unnecessary expense.

Most music publishing companies license their catalogs through an agency, such as the Harry Fox Agency, that handles song-request negotiations for a small fee. Congress has established a minimum mechanical royalty (an amount paid for the right to record the song of another), but an individual wishing to record someone else's song may negotiate a lower fee. While fee negotiations for the use of a song on an album do not normally require the services of a lawyer, legal services are helpful for fee negotiations on licensing music for commercials, television programs, or movie soundtracks, and licensing for special programming.

Television stations normally pay the performing rights societies (BMI, ASCAP, SESAC) a blanket licensing fee for the right to use all the songs in their catalogues but the individual producer of a program must secure a master use license from the record company to use the sound recording and a synchronization license to use the underlying words and music.

Lawyers working with music publishers basically perform contract negotiations or litigation and both functions require an extensive background in copyright law. Behind the government, the performing rights societies are the second largest group of plaintiffs in the federal court system.

A Law School Internship Leads to a Career

Sam worked as a lawyer for one of the two largest music-publishing companies in the world. He worked at the company headquarters in Los Angeles until the company was spun-off and sold.

Sam attended law school in Los Angeles so that he could take advantage of the entertainment law internships offered by the school. During the summer following his first year, Sam worked as an intern in the legal department of the publishing company. At the end of the summer, Sam stayed in his position as a volunteer and continued to volunteer at the company during his entire law school career. He learned as much about the company and the function of the legal department as he could, and took on as much responsibility as he could, making himself a part of the department.

When Sam graduated from law school, he asked for a full-time job, surprising some of the staff members who thought he already had a job. Sam's volunteer strategy had worked. Over the past two years he had integrated himself into the department and had become an indispensable member of the team. Sam was the first and only intern at the company who turned his internship into a full-time job, and recommends internships as a way to learn about potential employers and meet people who can introduce law students to potential employers.

Sam primarily reviewed music licenses and researched the chain of title for songs in their catalogue. He did not negotiate the licenses as a member of the legal department; license negotiation was handled by a different department. His client is the company so he does negotiate contract language with the lawyers for the particular song or songwriter that is the subject of the deal. Since the company does not do anything but music publishing, Sam thinks he is ready for a change. After the company was sold, Sam was able to use his experience to join an entertainment law firm as a partner.

CONCLUSION

There are dozens of different positions in the music industry for which a lawyer's special skills in negotiating contracts and knowledge of copyright law are valuable assets, whether the lawyer works for an entertainment law firm, as an in-house counsel, or for individual artists. There are many paths to finding a satisfying career in this field, as these profiles illustrate, and while luck may be part of that first break, hard work and long hours are surely part of staying power. As long as the supply of entertainment lawyers outnumbers those who can afford them, most lawyers choosing this specialty would be wise to have another area of law to supplement their income until that day when they become a name in the industry themselves.

Chapter 4

THEATER

Legitimate theater has always required the special services of entertainment lawyers familiar with the unique problems involved in staging a theatrical production. These requirements range from securing the rights to perform a play to negotiating contracts with the investors, producers, writers, directors, actors, and set designers. They include complying with union standards for set design and construction, lighting and ushers, and guild requirements for directors, actors and extras. Lawyers also play an important role in negotiating rights to music, venue rental, and insurance.

For the most part, theater specialists are clustered in New York City. A very few are located in Los Angeles, San Francisco, Chicago, and other major metropolitan areas where theater is beginning to expand to meet the demand for live theatrical entertainment. Often, several lawyers with expertise in one or more of the required areas will work together to complete a theatrical production deal.

Clients can vary from an investment group seeking to purchase the rights to a play to the playwright attempting to place his or her work with a production group. The section on the Dramatists Guild in Chapter 8 includes additional information on representing playwrights. After the initial property is purchased, negotiations for the actual presentation begins. Initial negotiations include the rental of a rehearsal hall for cast rehearsals. Many productions begin in satellite cities where the play can be tested before it moves on-Broadway. Los Angeles/Pasadena and Boston are two of the cities where producers will test a play to gauge the audience's reaction to the story and cast. The producers make their changes based on the audience's feedback. When the show is ready for primetime, the producers take the show to Broadway.

Most directors and actors receive a union-guaranteed minimum fee. They are free to negotiate for more than the minimum if their name attracts people to the production. Name producers, directors, and actors, along with the playwright, normally receive a set fee for their services plus points in the production.

Points are a percentage of the gross or net proceeds from the production. Theatrical contracts often contain several pages defining the gross or net proceeds from which the individual in question will receive his or her points. Performers receive one amount for rehearsal and a greater amount for the actual stage performance.

While the performers are being auditioned and placed under contract, a set designer and costume designer need to be hired so their work can begin. The theater or venue must be secured and insurance coverage negotiated before the show can open. This behind-the-scenes legal work can take months of preparation and negotiation.

All parties involved—investors, producers, directors, name actors, guilds and unions, and theater and insurance companies—have lawyers for their individual contract negotiation. While the insurance companies, venue, guilds, and unions may have in-house or retained council, the other parties will hire established lawyers in the field.

GETTING ESTABLISHED

Word-of-mouth is the best method of attracting clients in the entertainment field. Clients feel more comfortable hiring a lawyer with a background and a good reputation in the field than they do taking a chance on an unknown lawyer. In high stakes negotiations, clients are willing to pay for the best lawyers in the field.

The majority of lawyers representing theatrical clients bill their clients by the hour. Some charge an hourly rate plus points while others work for points alone. Again, the definition of the net from which a lawyer will receive his or her share is subject to negotiation. The client also needs a lawyer to represent him or her in the lawyer-client representation contract negotiations. Fee arrangements are dictated by the lawyer's and client's clout in the industry. The greater the client's reputation, the more rights he or she will be able to retain. Individuals with marquee value are able to negotiate a greater percentage of the box office gross than lesser-known individuals. Theatrical production point participation can be extremely risky based on production expenses and depending upon the definition of gross and net proceeds. It can also be very rewarding.

Experience with an established theatrical lawyer is the best way to begin a career in this specialty area. Working with one of the guilds is another stepping stone to a career as a theatrical lawyer. Virtually no client will hire an inexperienced lawyer when so much money is at stake. Referrals based on a reputation earned from experience are the way to become successful in the field.

Chapter 5

Like the recording industry, the film industry offers a variety of positions for lawyers. They may work for a firm that specializes in this field or as a solo practitioner. Lawyers are also hired by the studios and unions. Individual film stars, once they are clearly established, will have their own lawyer, but there are thousands of aspiring actors and actresses who need a lawyer's expertise.

FILM STUDIOS

All major motion picture studios have in-house legal departments to handle the day-to-day legal work of property acquisition, story and music copyrights, talent negotiations, and guild agreement compliance with actors, extras, directors, licensing, and distribution. Outside counsel is usually retained for litigation and complex business transactions. Studios normally seek medium- to large-size law firms when retaining outside counsel because these firms are more capable of providing the specific expertise along with the support staff to successfully represent the studio's interest.

Most studios do not hire recent law school graduates because they are not equipped to train new associates. Exceptions have been made in instances where the individual has worked for the studio as an intern during law school. But even when the student has worked for the studio as a paid legal assistant, the studios would rather hire someone with two or more years of experience in the substantive specialty area where the studio has a need. This policy allows the studio to hire someone who is qualified to begin work immediately rather than spend a lot of valuable time in training.

The following personal profiles are illustrative of the career path followed by studio executives in major motion picture studios. Their career paths are fairly typical of colleagues in similar positions.

Profile of a Labor Relations Lawyer

Nalinya is a lawyer in the Labor Relations department at a major theme park resort. Her job requires her to negotiate collective bargaining agreements, interpret policy for operators, and handle the employee disciplinary cases for the company. The resort has approximately 20,000 employees. Eighty percent of the employees are represented by one of thirty-two unions. There are sixteen different collective bargaining agreements governing their wages and working conditions. Her typical day consists of defending the company against union grievances, discussing collective bargaining issues with various lines of business leaders, providing operations advice to the managers in the field, preparing for arbitrations, and negotiations with union representatives.

When Nalinya graduated from law school, she had planned on using her International Law Certificate to practice international human rights law with a non-profit National Governing Organization. After her attempts to secure a job within the field, she took a vacation to visit her sister in Los Angeles. After a few weeks, she took a temporary job at Universal Music Group, which launched her entertainment law career. From there, she took a job at the Screen Actors Guild. After a few years with SAG, she had worked with a top five advertising agency in their Business Affairs department, a major television production studio in legal affairs, and she founded her own entertainment contracts consulting company. Her labor law and legal affairs expertise has helped all of the companies where she has worked to save money by avoiding union claims for failure to comply with the various guild agreements.

Nalinya loves the constant learning that is required to keep up with the various labor agreements she is required to know in order to perform her duties. She loves working with the various constituencies involved with the diverse problems that arise from employing 20,000 people. The occasional unpleasant interactions with labor union business representatives are infrequent enough so as to not dampen her enthusiasm for the job.

Nalinya recommends that you need to develop a substantive expertise related to the entertainment industry so that your expertise satisfies a company's need. Also, don't be afraid to take a job that doesn't pay very much in the beginning to develop an expertise. Relationships are key. It is also important to be persistent and not easily discouraged. There is a lot of competition for entertainment industry jobs. Nalinya found her current job online at Indeed.com. She then applied through the general website. Her persistence has paid off.

Profile of a Studio Executive in the Legal Department

Dick has practiced entertainment law with an emphasis in copyright for more than thirty-five years. After graduating from an eastern law school, he began work in a private law firm in New York. During his four years at the firm, Dick met the head of the legal department of a major motion picture studio. Because the studio's lawyers had been impressed with his work, they hired him for their copyright department. Over the years, his general corporate duties included real estate acquisition, litigation, antitrust, feature motion picture production matters, distribution, music publishing and recording, foreign and domestic contract negotiations, and copyright.

Dick worked for the studio for nine years before he was hired by a rival studio in New York. At his new job, he concentrated on general feature motion picture production matters, litigation, music publishing and recording, copyright, merchandising, and foreign and domestic contract negotiations. His work required trips to Los Angeles, London, and Paris.

After four years, Dick was hired by a Los Angeles entertainment conglomerate as assistant general counsel. His duties included corporate broadcasting operations, real estate, construction, litigation, and franchising in addition to his television and feature motion picture production work, entertainment packaging, network and syndication contracts, FCC matters, copyrights, music publishing, and recording contract negotiations. After seven years at that company, he was hired by another major international entertainment conglomerate. Following a short stint with the new company, he returned to the motion picture company where he had spent four years in New York and worked in the legal department at the company's corporate headquarters in Los Angeles.

Dick spent the last nine years of his career at the studio, supervising the distribution and marketing lawyers and all foreign and domestic copyright submissions. Because of his expertise in copyright he was summoned by Congress to testify on the 1976 Copyright Act. His position required a great deal of travel to and from New York, with an occasional trip to Europe. Today, Dick has retired from the studio, and teaches entertainment law and copyright law part-time at a southern California law school.

Dick says he enjoyed the opportunities offered by working for corporations, but in retrospect, he thinks he could have had similar experiences and made more money working in a law firm. While he enjoyed the advantages of a corporate job with relatively regular working hours, he missed some of the camaraderie that his friends and classmates, including a former President of the United States, had enjoyed. If he had to do it over again, Dick says he would only have worked for a studio for a few years and then returned to a law firm to finish his career.

Dick recommends that students interested in entertainment law learn as much about the industry as possible as well as excelling academically during law school. There is no substitute for knowledge after getting that first break, he says.

Portrait of Studio Legal and Business Affairs Executives

Richard finally realized his dream to work in the entertainment industry after years of trying to find an in-house position.

Richard graduated at the top of his law school class. While he wanted to work for a studio when he graduated from law school, he did not have the practice experience the studios needed from their lawyers. Richard had several offers from very large law firms in Los Angeles. He accepted a job at one and worked in their transactional department for two years. Richard did not like the long hours that were expected of all of the associates at the firm so he started to look for another position. He couldn't find an in-house position at a studio, so he decided to put his dream on hold and move to San Diego.

Richard moved into the transactional department at one of the large San Diego law firms. His law firm was involved with large corporate mergers and acquisitions as well as general corporate representation. In addition to his regular corporate clients, Richard worked to expand his client list to include local entertainment companies. As he attracted local television and radio station clients, his desire to work for a studio in Los Angeles was rekindled.

Richard kept in touch with his classmates who had stayed in Los Angeles following graduation. They told him about every opening they heard about on the street. He read the trade papers every day for job postings. Richard answered an advertisement for a position as a lawyer at a major studio. He had applied for the same job four years earlier, after he had graduated from law school, but he had been turned down because he didn't have any legal experience. This time, he had the experience the studio was looking for. The senior lawyer remembered Richard and hired him for an entry-level position in the studio's international department. Although he took a significant pay cut to take the position, Richard enjoyed his new job because he got to work on complex legal problems that resulted in a tangible piece of intellectual property. "It is a great feeling to watch a movie knowing that you contributed to the final product. While the filmmakers wouldn't consider our work a contribution to the final product, they couldn't work if we didn't do a lot of behind-the-scenes work to make it possible for them to create. I wish I would have gotten here sooner, but it all worked out in the end. I love it here."

After a few years with the studio, Richard decided that reading the same contracts over and over was no longer stimulating. He had moved up in the legal department, but believed that he had climbed as high as he could because the lawyers in the higher positions were relatively young, content, and not likely to move on. Richard started looking around for a more challenging position. He found an opportunity with a start-up cable company and decided to take a chance on the company.

The job required Richard to move to the company headquarters, which provided cleaner air and a more reasonable cost of living than Los Angeles. Richard helped build the company from a start-up to one of the top cable movie channels. Over the years, he was promoted to Senior Vice President for Business and Legal Affairs. At that position, headhunters contacted him regularly offering opportunities to move. After many years at the cable company, he took the same position at an independent film company so that he could be closer to the actual creation of the content that he had been licensing for his previous company. From there, he became a corporate consultant for a company involved in media acquisitions. He loves his job and particularly loves living in Colorado. He travels to New York and Los Angeles regularly.

Persistence and Hard Work Pay Off

Christa attended Pepperdine University for her bachelors, masters, and law degrees. After graduating with a BA in Economics and a BS in Business Administration, she worked at a studio in the finance department as a financial analyst. She quit work to get her MBA and JD degrees. After taking the bar, she started looking for work in the entertainment industry. Except for the people she met in the finance department at the studio, she didn't know anyone in the industry, so she cold-called studio lawyers from an alumni list to request informational interviews. In addition, she reached out to anyone she knew who knew someone in the entertainment industry so that she could secure more informational interviews. She always kept the interviews brief to respect the interviewee's time. She listened intently, sent handwritten thank-you notes, and followed up with the recommendations she received from the interviews. After speaking and meeting with numerous people, she landed her first job in entertainment.

Christa's first job was "too good to be true." She started work as the sole in-house counsel for the co-owner and co-creator of a company that was sold for $2.5 billion shortly after she arrived. While she was there, she "had the privilege of working . . . under the leadership of one of the most prolific lawyers in the business, Howard Weitzman." Among others, Mr. Weitzman "represents the Estate of Michael Jackson, Justin Bieber, the Kardashians, Sharon Osbourne, and was the lead lawyer in the *DeLorean* trials." "I was only in-house counsel to him with respect to his new venture after he sold King World – he just wouldn't pull the trigger on the new venture," so Christa began an uncomfortably long search for a new job.

"Finally, after living off my credit cards for a good amount of time, I checked my ego at the door and worked as a part-time assistant at a small entertainment law firm; I got my hands on everything I possibly could, devouring every word of every contract, asking the lawyers [to allow me] to listen in on all calls and [to] attempt to draft their docs for them." Her hard work paid off. Christa was next hired as an in-house lawyer by one of the firm's clients at a film production company. Once she went in-house, she worked hard to impress her bosses. Again and again, her hard work paid off as she was pursued by headhunters and other studios. Each time she changed jobs, it was for more responsibility within the company. She is now an Executive Vice President and Head of Business Affairs at a prestigious independent film company.

When asked about a typical day in the life, Christa said, "I spin at my gym early mornings, or if we're very busy at work and I need to make international calls, I'll skip it and come in early to reach our international contacts before they head home for the evening. This will often involve negotiating outstanding points on foreign distribution rights on one of our films, for example. Throughout the day, I'm responding to countless e-mails and calls ... involving our productions, legal advisement, negotiations of talent deals, and financial questions and contract interpretation questions from accounting, producers, and others. I'm lucky if there isn't at least one heated/contentious call/e-mail. I have business lunches with colleagues daily (unless I cancel because I'm too busy, such as now, as we just started production on our new film).

"Let me give you today, for example: I came in early to reach the UK regarding a book-publishing tie-in negotiation for our upcoming (hopefully Oscar bound) film, *12 Years a Slave;* I also have to manage our UK distributor with respect to this deal. Next, I had to prepare my response to Cusack's reps with respect to a very protracted negotiation of his backend (contingent compensation) on our current film; this included my looking up a couple of past stars' backends on our last two films to confirm I could not only justify my counter by reasoning/logic but also by indicating that 'if it's good enough for Pitt and Penn, it should be good enough for you' (Thus, I had to verify this). I just finished a conference call with our insurer's attorney ... and the writer of our screenplay in reference to a demand letter regarding our script, strategizing how we would respond, if at all.

"For the remainder of the day, I'll need to have a couple of calls with various guilds, as there always seems to be some issue with one of the guilds no matter how upright/above board a company [we are]. I need to review the redrafts of the two outstanding foreign distribution long-form agreements on *12 Years a Slave.* I will need to review and comment upon many agreements relating to services on this film we're currently shooting ...specifically, I need to read and comment upon the producer's long form agreement. I need to return Giamatti's reps' call to argue about outstanding points on his deal. I have a production meeting, where I'll advise others upon the status of various business items including the status of the bond. I have two computer screens, so on one of them, I'm reviewing dailies of our film to see if I note any major clearance issues, in the background while I work and answer emails. I have a Board of Directors meeting tonight from 6:00 to 9:00, and then I'll relax a bit at home before falling into bed."

Christa has the following advice to anyone interested in breaking into the entertainment industry: "If you are passionate about it and you 'need' it in your bones, you'll be just fine. It's tough to break in, but if you have the stamina and are persistent (and like I had to, check your ego at the door), it will happen. Talk to as many people as possible, finding out who knows someone who's in the business that you can sit down with and ask advice and learn about their story (and who else they might refer you to).

"Where do you want to work? Research the companies of interest to you and cold call them; while it may sound scary, there are worse things, and it works.

"Read the 'trades' online (*Daily Variety* and *Hollywood Reporter*), so that you're versed in various topics of the business.

"Listen well and be honest—don't pretend like you know what you're doing or what we do; you don't, and we can tell."

INDEPENDENT FILM

Independent filmmakers range from extremely successful production companies with studio lot deals to film students trying to break into the business. Independent filmmakers need legal work whether they can afford it or not. The risks of making a film without legal representation are too great.

Most independent filmmakers do not have in-house counsel. The established filmmakers have lawyers they have been working with for years. New filmmakers are constantly looking for competent representation for a reasonable price. Some filmmakers are willing to give a lawyer a percentage of the profits in exchange for legal work, but remember the discussion of Eddie Murphy's "monkey points" before you agree to get paid with a percentage of the net. You may end up being a volunteer providing a lot of free legal work.

Independent filmmakers have the same issues that studios have. Among other things, the independent filmmaker must secure the rights to the intellectual property (script), hire actors (possible SAG issues) and crew (possible issues with the stagehand union), secure locations (state and local film permits), rent all of the equipment necessary to shoot the film, and house and feed the actors and crew.

An Avocation Becomes a Vocation

William has been a performer all his life. He has a picture of himself performing in a first grade Easter production. He was in his Boy Scout Drum & Bugle Corps, performed in theater at his high school, and took guitar lessons as a teenager. He participated in theater during college while majoring in English Literature. He went straight through college and law school to defer his induction into the Army during the Vietnam War. After law school, he joined the Army where he served in the JAG Corps for five years. William continued to act in the Army theater program and won an award for the Best Actor for his role in *Of Mice and Men*. After leaving the JAG Corps, William became a prosecutor back in his hometown. After spending a few years in the State Attorney's office, William was approached by a transactional firm that needed a litigator. He left the prosecutor's office and joined a private law firm.

In the mid-1980s, William's martial arts instructor made a movie. In addition to being in the movie, William handled the legal work for the very low budget independent film. The happenstance of acting in the movie and working as the lawyer for the production company made William realize that he could merge his avocation with his profession.

After experiencing success as a litigator in the private sector, William left and formed his own firm. He met musicians and actors who provided him with referrals. While most of the new clients could not afford to pay a lawyer, they referred clients who eventually could afford to pay.

One of William's clients had a production office on the Disney property. William moved his office to the Disney property to be close to the client. The move opened doors for William to meet new potential clients. After spending time on the Disney lot, he moved his office to the Universal Studios Producers building. He began producing movies as well as servicing clients in both the film and music business. While on the Universal lot, he became friends with some independent producers who he felt were extremely creative. When they proposed a low-budget film, William helped them raise money for production as well as served as the lawyer on the project. *The Blair Witch Project* was a career changer for the filmmakers and William. Shortly after that, William was able to quit taking on non-entertainment clients. William says it is feast or famine as far as legal and production work goes, but he loves his work and wouldn't change a thing.

It's My Passion!

Anita always wanted to be in the entertainment industry. As an undergraduate at Emory University, she coupled her Marketing, Consulting, and Venture Management major with a Dance and Movement Studies minor. After graduation, she moved to Los Angeles to pursue her dancing career and, as a professional dancer, she appeared in music videos and local shows, including the MTV Video Music Production Awards show. However, as much as Anita loved to perform, she understood the realities of life as a dancer and decided to merge her interests and abilities by pursuing a career in entertainment law.

Anita looked at law schools all across the country and decided on the University of Miami because of its entertainment program and its joint JD-MBA program. While in law school, she participated in the ABA Law Student Division's Negotiation Competition, the Intellectual Property Law Society, and served on the school's Entertainment and Sports Law Society's executive committee. One summer during law school, she worked for White and Case, LLP in Singapore. She was extended an offer to return the next summer but chose to work as an unpaid intern at Warner Music Latin America in Miami instead. During her final year in school, White and Case made her an offer that she declined so that she could pursue her dream to be an entertainment lawyer. As graduation approached, she knew she needed to choose between New York and Los Angeles to begin her career. She hoped to take advantage of her East Coast connections and decided to take the New York bar.

After taking the bar, finding a job was seemingly impossible. It was 2009, no one was hiring, and the firms that were wanted lawyers with experience. To keep active in the legal community, Anita volunteered as an intern at a theater company in Brooklyn where she reviewed contracts and venue agreements, and taught for Kaplan as a bar preparation guide to supplement her income.

Around March, an opening came up at Stuart Weitzman (a New York fashion house specializing in shoes and handbags), and she seemed to fit their current needs perfectly: "(1) I was open to working as an unpaid intern . . . , (2) I had some [mergers and acquisitions] experience due to my work at White & Case (Stuart Weitzman was being acquired by Jones Apparel Group at the time), and (3) I was willing to work as many hours as they needed me. Barbara Kolsun, the General Counsel at Stuart Weitzman, became a valued mentor and introduced me to all of her professional contacts. I interviewed at several fashion houses and IP firms, none of whom were looking to hire a first year [lawyer]. Through Barbara's contacts, I met with a partner at a reputable law firm with a strong Media and IP practice. He told me very frankly that they couldn't hire me, but that he would happily put me in touch with his college roommate, Josh Sandler, who was practicing entertainment law at the time." I had an informational interview with Josh who told me that the firm he was working with, Gray Krauss Stratford Des Rochers, was looking for an associate with three to five years of experience. Nonetheless, he put my resume in the pile and I made my passion for entertainment law very clear at the first interview. I offered to work for free until I proved my worth to them. Seven interviews later, they gave me a chance. And now, three years later, I am still happily working at the firm.

"Typically, I'm in the office from 9:00 a.m. until 8:00 p.m. Sometimes I come in earlier and leave later. On any given day, I'm usually working on between five and eight films that are in production and several others in the development or delivery stages. On average I put in a 1/2 day either on Saturday or Sunday. Oftentimes I leave work and head to a screening or client's event, maybe one or two per week. I've attended the Sundance Film Festival for the past three years (all of the film attorneys here attend), been to South by Southwest, the Toronto International Film Festival and, of course, the Tribeca Film Festival. Last year we represented sixteen films at Sundance, and had eighteen the year before. Each of the attorneys spends about a week at Sundance, with some of the partners staying longer if a film gets picked up for distribution.

"I love the collaborative approach of representing production companies and producers. As production counsel, we handle everything from optioning the underlying rights to a script, drafting all production-related agreements (actors, director, director of photography, production designer, etc.), engaging a sales agent and finally, negotiating the terms of distribution. We are involved with various clearance-related matters, as well as location agreements and product releases; basically, "soup to nuts" of production. Through the months of work on any given project, we really gain a sense of ownership over the film. Once we get to see the film in its entirety, the whole package of work comes together visually, which is amazing to see. I love having an emotional connection to my work...I don't think many lawyers can say that."

"The daily stresses of production can really cause anxiety for some of our clients and they can get a little pushy for work to get done 'ASAP, ASAP, ASAP.' There's also always a bit of hand-holding through various issues (both minor and substantial). For the most part, however, our clients are seasoned veterans and don't 'cry wolf' too often.

"Our office setting is unique for a law firm (including entertainment law firms). We are partnered with a post-production studio, so our office space includes editing suites, screening rooms, and an ADR (voiceover) room. This means we share space with editors, actors, and directors on a daily basis, not to mention that we have two producers who share office space on a permanent basis. This allows us, as lawyers, to be around the forces that create some of our projects."

Anita said that her contracts course was the most helpful for her current activities. Her copyright class was useful, but it was much more expansive that the concepts she applies on a daily basis. The entertainment related classes she took have not necessarily helped her with her current job, but certainly drove her to pursue her passion further. Anita said that if you really want to follow your passion, do everything you can to network. Attend CLE programs and meet the speakers and other attendees, even those starting out at the same level as you. Understanding the entertainment industry is as important as understanding the law; clients want to be advised by someone who speaks their language. Membership in the California and New York bars is a must. Anita hopes to be living in Los Angeles working for the same firm in the near future. Getting more involved in the creative aspects of production, or producing a film, is in her future.

UNIONS

There are many professional associations and guilds that protect those who work in the film industry. There are the larger, well-known organizations, such as the American Guild of Variety Artists (AGVA) and the Screen Actors Guild (SAG), and smaller, more specialized groups, such as Women in Film and the Alliance for Gay and Lesbian Artists in the Entertainment Industry. There are separate associations for those who work in every phase of film production, including those who write, film, edit, direct, and produce. There is the Stuntmen's Association of Motion Pictures, the Stuntwomen's Association of Motion Pictures, the Black Stuntmen's Association, and the International Stunt Association. A list of some of the industry organizations can be found in Appendix B.

Like other professional associations, these various groups are the voice for their members. They work to protect their interests through bargaining agreements and setting standards. They may lobby for legislation at the national or state level and may litigate cases that affect members or play a supporting role in litigation on their behalf. The following Diary of a Union Executive illustrates the type of work these organizations are involved in on a day-to-day basis.

A Union Executive's Diary

Bob is a former performer who now works as the executive secretary for a major industry union. As the chief administrative executive of the union based in the New York City headquarters, Bob is responsible for hiring and firing employees, preparing the union's budget, conducting board meetings, directing the executive staff in contract enforcement actions, and negotiating the collective bargaining agreement.

Bob graduated from a state university with a Bachelor of Arts degree. He obtained a Master of Arts degree in dramatic arts from a Midwestern university. He worked for twenty years as a performer before returning to school for a law degree.

After law school he worked as a business representative for an artist's equity association for two years before becoming the executive secretary for the union. Bob has held his current position for over fourteen years.

Bob travels between New York and Los Angeles every quarter because the union has a branch office in Los Angeles. All of the staff lawyers who work for the union are members of either the New York or California bar, and some are members of both. The general counsel works out of the New York office with Bob. A staff lawyer is assigned to the Los Angeles office.

As a prerequisite for practice in the field, Bob stresses the importance of understanding the business side of entertainment. Courses in labor relations, contracts, agency, and remedies are helpful preparation while in school. A solid academic background coupled with an understanding of the "business" are essential for success in the industry, according to Bob.

To illustrate the tasks that Bob performs every day, he generously offered his daily diary. He reports that this is a typical month's schedule. The diary has been *minimally* edited for space considerations.

Monday

9:30 Review last two months' correspondence of department heads.

10:00 Consult with department head re: television promo grievance.

10:30 Review incoming mail for the day.

11:00 Consult with agency department head re: talent commissions for an agent's successor.

11:30 Dictate letter to Immigration and Naturalization Service objecting to H-I visa for British stunt coordinator.

12:00 Consult with editor of branch newsletter on the lead story. Counsel board member on travel plans for negotiation session.

12:30 Phone call to trade paper to warn about unfavorable comment on radio show.

1:00 Review past months' correspondence of department head and executive assistant to advisor department head.

1:30 Consult with assistant in Industrial Department re: (1) rulings and staffing; (2) collection arbitration awards.

2:00 Lunch

3:00 Consult with department head concerning jurisdiction for Philippine feature coverage for International TV films.

3:30 Write reply to member seeking Union's endorsement of housing project.

4:00 Review correspondence of affirmative action administrator. Consult with and advise office manager about performance evaluation forms.

4:30 Meet with my secretary to rearrange filing, schedules, etc.

Tuesday

10:30 Meet with real estate agents to discuss counteroffer on new office.

11:00 Cost is higher than anticipated. Decide to present counteroffer to committee.

11:30 Quick meetings with secretary and department heads for go-aheads, etc.

12:00 Review executive assistant's January correspondence. Skim trade papers.

12:30 Consult with affirmative action administrator on coordination of video project.

1:00 Teleconference of national executive commission with affiliated union.

2:00 Travel to Los Angeles.

Wednesday–Friday

In Los Angeles for Industrial Negotiations

Monday

9:30 Meet with theatrical/TV department head for update on employee problem. Employee refuses to report schedule. Decide to talk to her.

10:30 Quick meeting with office manager on scheduling. Speak to agency department head concerning scheduling of disciplinary hearing.

11:30 Meet with agency department head about rights of former agent when actor goes to another agent.

12:00 Meet with newsletter editor to review galleys and add notice on industrial negotiator breakdown.

12:30 Draft and correct letter to leading players emphasizing need to receive reports when child actor is mistreated.

1:00 Lunch

2:30 Speak to national executive secretary concerning additional vacation for staff.

3:00 Agree to add 3 days and to announce to staff tomorrow.

3:30 Meet with office manager to discuss implications and details of additional vacation. Drafted memos to exempt and nonexempt staff.

Tuesday

9:30 Meet with agency department head of personnel.

10:00 Phone editor of newsletter with changes and suggestions on galleys.

10:30 Meet with secretary for dictation and filing.

11:00 Meet with employee to resolve her objections to reporting by phone from sets. Decide to meet again tomorrow with theatrical/TV department head.

12:00 Dictation and filing

2:30 Phone call to Los Angeles executives to discuss deferred agenda from last week's San Diego board meeting.

3:00 Consult with branch member about her proposed article on "colorization" of films.

3:30 Lunch

4:30 Meet with member to discuss sweepstakes and complaints.

Wednesday

9:30 Meet with office manager to finalize language on employee performance evaluation forms.

10:00 Meet with affirmative action administrator to discuss agenda for EEOC conference in Washington, D.C.

10:30 Meet with agency department head to discuss disciplining agent for sending members for non-union jobs.

11:00 Meet with membership department supervisor about agent complaint.

11:30 Meet with theatrical/TV head to clear reporting problems.

12:00 Met with employee on refusal to report schedule. We agree on reporting—records to be kept by supervisor. Attitude to be worked on. Field representatives to get reports on same day.

2:00 Lunch

2:30 Meet with real estate agents on new office space proposal.

3:00 Meet with associate national executive secretary on Teamster's Los Angeles extra players deal and further information on Los Angeles board meeting.

4:00 Quick consultation with theater/TV department head to inform of Teamsters deal.

4:30 Advise executive assistant in commercial department on canceled negotiation deal.

5:00 Meet with New York president and associate national executive secretary for update and prepare for New York executive committee [New York union officers] meeting tomorrow.

Thursday

9:30 Quick meeting with associate national executive secretary—strategy for next meeting.

10:00 Meet with field representatives' associate national executive secretary, theatrical/TV head about field representatives' car leasing and being a separate department. Look further into leasing.

11:00 Meet with industrial department head about interpretation of industrial contract and vacation policy for employees.

11:30 Meet with member to discuss industrial negotiations.

12:00 Follow-up with field representatives' supervisor.

12:30 Meet with office manager to get spring meeting location.

1:00 Meet with agency department head about agent refusing to participate in access program. Decide to discuss with association national executive secretary.

1:30 New York executive commission meeting: 1) Approve lease negotiations on new offices; 2) Update on affiliated union deal; 3) Approve performers w/ disabilities dollar request.

2:30 Meet with union counsel and associate national executive secretary to discuss affiliated union deal and NFL players' brief on merchandising the videotapes of NFL games.

4:30 Attend union-sponsored Black History event.

Friday

9:30 Quick conference with agency, affirmative action, and theatrical/TV department heads on pending cases.

10:30 Dictate memo to members advising of affiliated union–Teamster deal.

11:00 Meet with associate national executive secretary about possible comp time off for secretary due to transit strike.

11:30 Meet with office manager to discuss photos of conservatory, seminars, and demeanor for secretaries who are idle.

12:00 Edit draft of proposed industrial contract.

12:30 Approve and countersign checks for bills for New York branch.

2:00 National executive commission teleconference—wording of dues referendum.

5:30 Teleconference with comptroller, national executive secretary, and the association's national executive secretary covering 1) travel reimbursement policy and 2) car repair policy.

Monday

Office Holiday

Tuesday

9:30 Review *The New York Times* article on New York smoking ban—give to office manager for recommendations.

10:00 Meet with affirmative action administrator for update. Review Western section minutes.

10:30 Review proposed personnel policy manual.

11:00 Telephone conference with industrial department head

11:30 Review day's mail and sign correspondence.

12:00 Dictate memos on performance evaluation process.

12:30 Meet with office manager to discuss information on dues restructuring referendum.

3:00 Meet with commercial department head and office manager to discuss employee "down time" behavior. Decide to talk with other department heads as well.

4:30 Meet to report and discuss negotiation breakdown.

Wednesday

9:30 Build agenda and kit for Eastern section board meeting.

10:00 Distribute changes in affirmative action forms for theatrical/TV agreements.

10:30 Telephone—discuss relocation with realtor and architect.

11:00 Meet with theatrical/TV department head re: right-to-work restriction on film in Los Angeles.

11:30 Review correspondence and trade papers.

12:00 Draft memo to staff explaining referendum on dues and initiation fees.

1:30 Meet with theater/TV department head on microfilming—reviewing old arbitrations.

3:00 Teleconference with assistant national associate executive secretary concerning agenda for staff conference.

5:00 Meet with associate national executive secretary re: referendum language on dues increase and various staff matters.

Thursday

9:30 Meet with associate national executive secretary and board member to plan commercials.

10:00 Dictation and filing. Commence microfilm culling with secretary.

10:30 Review correspondence.

11:00 Observe field representatives meeting.

1:30 Meet with affirmative action administrator—Discuss union position on children in industrials.

2:00 Teleconference of national executive committee—wording of dues referendum.

4:30 Meet with stunt committee co-chairs and associate national executive secretary re: accident report.

5:30 Teleconference with Los Angeles staff on referendum language.

Friday

9:30 Meet with theatrical/TV department head—updates on various claims.

10:30 Review correspondence and trade papers.

11:00 Meet with theatrical/TV department head and office manager re: secretarial business.

11:30 Meet with industrial organizer re: joint board meeting on industrial negotiations.

12:00 Telephone conference with agency department on actor's change of agent—over to first agent's file.

12:30 Meet with agency department head.

2:00 Telephone conference with casting director—rates for TV.

2:30 Meet with theatrical/TV department head.

3:00 Executive staff meeting: review difficult cases and upgrades for commercials.

Tuesday

10:00 Meet with commercials department claims manager—explanation of member's anger over late claim. Advise to cover with letter in future.

11:00 Telephone affiliated union: check new building. Meet with secretary—correspondence and filing.

11:30 Meet with affirmative action administrator: update on report for board meeting and correspondence.

12:00 Review files list for microfilming.

1:30 Telephone call from Guild—claim for upgrade of extra players.

2:00 Meet with legislative committee chair—write letters re: unemployment department layoffs.

2:30 Meet with President—prepare for tonight's board meeting.

3:30 Meet with board member—complaints about photography policy at conservatory. Explained how to begin policy change through editorial board.

4:30 Meet with agency department head.

5:00 Joint board meeting—industrial contract department.

6:00 Eastern section board meeting.

12:00 The day finally ends.

Wednesday

10:00 Attend meeting of Council of Motion Picture and TV Unions.

10:30 General discussion of current issues common to East Coast unions.

1:00 Attend New York executive committee meeting to discuss working of referendum on dues.

2:00 Attend national executive commission teleconference on wording of referendum on dues.

Thursday

9:30 Review mail and trade papers.

10:00 Meet with Industrial Department to discuss travel ruling.

10:30 Meet with field representatives to announce referendum dates.

11:30 Meet with office manager to discuss relocation details.

1:00 Meet with architects and associate national executive secretary re: relocation status and details.

2:30 Meet with owner of new office space to finalize deal points.

Friday

10:00 Meet with associate national executive secretary about leafleting open call in referendum.

10:30 Meet with office manager re: leaflet content.

11:00 Review correspondence and trade papers.

11:30 Arrange travel to Los Angeles and San Diego for staff conference.

1:00 Meet with associate national executive secretary, agency department head and agents re: various agency regulations interpretations and procedures.

2:30 Review referendum language

3:00 Executive staff meeting

For Bob, the meetings seem to never end when dealing with so many constituencies. The diversity of the work keeps it exciting and fulfilling. Bob loves his work.

VIDEO GAMES

Video games are like movies in that they start with a script or story-board, include actors, and rely heavily on independent music to set the mood and keep the players interested. The game industry has both large corporate video game creators and independent game creators. Lawyers interested in working with video game companies need to be well versed in the same issues that confront other entertainment companies. On the mundane side, there are corporate governance issues and human resource issues. On the creative side, there are intellectual property issues. There are copyright issues in the computer program or the video display and music rights. The decision to copyright the intellectual property or to patent the software is one that companies make on an individualized basis. Patent law is always a consideration with video game development. Trademark registrations are necessary for the company's and the individual game's name and marks. If the video game is based on an existing film, the video game rights must be secured from the film's copyright owner. There are clearance issues if any products or other famous marks are included in the game. If celebrity voices are used, those contracts must be prepared. As more video games are turned into movies, those licensing agreements must be drafted.

Profile of a Video Game Lawyer

All through law school, Cheryl worked as an intern in her brother's law firm, which specialized in music clearances. Before he founded the firm, he had worked for a record company for the past few years. In addition to music clearances, the firm actively scouted for talented, unsigned bands. In an effort to expand their business, they began suggesting music from unsigned bands to video game developers. (Securing the rights to the music for a video game from an unsigned band requires less paperwork and costs less than the music from an established band.)

After a video game was released, a song from one of the firm's bands became a number one hit. The success of the band was directly tied to their song's placement in the video game. Suddenly, bands became interested in placing their music in video games for marketing purposes. Because of that success, Cheryl can now be very selective about the songs and bands' music that gets placed in a game. The cost of the music for the video game maker is considerably less than one would expect because the demand for placement far exceeds the need for music. Usually, Cheryl can negotiate a flat fee for the songs that get placed in a game. The benefit to the band is that their song is associated with a cool video game forever.

CONCLUSION

While the film industry employs many lawyers to negotiate the complex deals and licensing agreements, there are many more lawyers waiting for an opportunity to work in this field. Persistence pays off, and those with limited experience should consider volunteer or part-time work to bolster a resume. Knowing and understanding an organization and knowing staff in that organization will be assets when positions open up.

Chapter 6

Television involves many of the same legal issues as all of the other previously mentioned entertainment law specialties. A practitioner involved in television must be familiar with the other specialty areas because television involves securing the rights to scripts and hiring the producers, directors, actors, camera and lighting technicians, and all the other people who contribute to the on-air product. TV work also requires negotiating the rights to music, syndicating popular programs, securing movie and theatrical rights for special presentation, negotiating advertising contracts, labor union agreements, copyrights, and advising the news staff on sensitive issues. It involves a thorough understanding of business and labor relations as well as entertainment law.

The major networks have legal departments in both their Los Angeles and New York offices, but most of the in-house legal work is handled by the legal department at the network's headquarters. The majority of affiliate stations across the country, even in major markets, do not have in-house counsel. The major cable "superstations" do have small legal staffs.

Labor law specialists find a rich array of opportunities in television. In addition to working for a network, a labor lawyer could find work with one of the many unions and guilds that represent the professionals involved with television shows. Talent and directors each have guilds to represent them, as do the camera technicians, lighting technicians, set and prop builders, makeup artists, writers, reporters, and on-air news personnel.

Local union chapters will not have in-house counsel but generally retain a firm to assist in contract enforcement and negotiations. In addition to union work, many "name" individuals will retain outside counsel to assist them in negotiating rights and compensation beyond the minimum. Work hours, compensation, and fringe benefits vary depending on the situation in which a lawyer finds himself or herself. The following vignettes illustrate the differences.

Profile of a Network Lawyer

Ron is the head of a network television station's legal department in Los Angeles. Most of the network's lawyers are based in New York, but the Los Angeles office has a three-person general counsel legal staff, a labor relations department with three lawyers, and a business affairs office with a few lawyers who no longer practice. A total of thirty in-house lawyers work for the network in New York and Los Angeles.

Ron obtained his BA in political science and his LLB before moving to Los Angeles to work at one of the nation's largest law firms. His five years with the firm were spent in trial work with an emphasis in business litigation. He moved from the law firm to the network where he has worked his way to the top of the legal department. To advance further, Ron explains, he would have to relocate to the headquarters office in New York City.

No lawyers are hired out of law school to work for the company, according to Ron. A minimum of two years of related experience is a prerequisite, and trial experience is beneficial. Labor lawyers are most frequently hired because the industry is so heavily unionized, although the network also hires tax and business lawyers with contract or copyright experience. The company also places a heavy emphasis on academic excellence in law school.

Ron frequently travels to San Francisco to visit the station the network owns and operates there. He makes a quarterly trip to New York and has traveled to Europe once in his nine years with the company.

The in-house legal department at the network works with the entertainment department, the news department, and business affairs to avoid potential legal problems. In addition to the preventive law they practice, the lawyers handle claims and defend the network in litigation. The legal department staff deal mainly with libel, privacy, copyright, and FCC Act issues. The labor relations department handles employee and union grievances, contract enforcement, and union negotiations. In this bi-coastal industry, the Labor Relations Department in the headquarters office in New York leads the union negotiations, but the head of the department in Los Angeles is a key participant.

While it is beyond the scope of the legal department's duties, Ron reports that employees will often come to them for personal advice. The lawyers do what they can to advise the employees, but beyond the preliminary advice rendered, they never get involved in the cases.

Ron does not make as much as the partners with the same years of experience at the firm he left, but he is well paid. In addition to his base salary, Ron receives a company car, stock options, and bonuses. Also, unlike his counterparts in private practice, Ron works nine-to-five with most weekends off. He is able to enjoy his paid vacations because his "client" can call others in the department when an urgent issue develops. Additional benefits of his position include the opportunity to get into television and movie production and a chance to move into network management. Production opportunities are extracurricular and not a part of his job.

After spending ten years at the network, Ron decided to rejoin his old firm as a partner. Ron decided to give up the perquisites for the money. He now serves as outside counsel for the network when the network decides to farm out some of its work.

Profile of a Private Practitioner

In contrast to Ron, who worked at the network, Ryan is a private practitioner in a five-lawyer firm in New York City. The firm, which he founded after working in various firms for twenty-five years, is primarily engaged in corporate mergers and acquisitions with a substantial civil litigation practice. Their entertainment work concentrates on negotiating television rights for sporting events and literary properties.

Four of the five lawyers in the firm do some entertainment law. Ryan spends most of his time representing entertainment clients. His clients include producers and directors, talent, and nonprofit organizations such as fine arts guilds.

Ryan attended a New York law school and began work as an associate in a twelve-person firm. His work included representing a newsreel and documentary producer where he negotiated with the union for talent and technicians. Over the years, he has represented film and documentary producers, advertising agencies, major sporting events and their producers, soap opera producers, the Miss America Pageant, authors, publishers, on-air television talent, agents, and professional golfers. Retirement is not an option as Ryan feels uncomfortable when he is not working, and vacations are secondary to his career demands.

Ryan travels extensively throughout the United States and the Far East for his clients, but the bulk of his work is concentrated in New York City. Ryan enjoys his work and doesn't mind the long hours, which include at least one weekend day a week.

Ryan's advice to students is similar to that of others in this field. "Learn the business, whether it is the television business, motion picture business, music business, publishing business, or sports business," he advises. "A good lawyer is a good lawyer, and to be a good entertainment lawyer you must first be a good lawyer. Specific skills can be acquired as you become familiar with the nuances of entertainment practice."

Profile of a Entrepreneurial Television Lawyer

Mona is the president of a business affairs company where she "advises clients working in film, television, digital media, and other types of entertainment on legal matters as well as business strategy and development opportunities. Most recently, she has been working on a variety of television projects for Nigel Lythgoe Productions and currently handles product integration and licensing agreements for the *Project Runway* series and other television series and films produced by The Weinstein Company. She currently consults for Summit Entertainment regarding their merchandising and licensing program and marketing and promotion activities for *The Twilight Saga* series of movies and other properties. She also handled Simon Fuller's groundbreaking digital web series, *If I Can Dream,* which created challenging legal issues due to its round-the-clock live digital feed of the participants."

Prior to establishing her own business, Mona served as Vice President, Business Affairs at Dick Clark Productions, Inc. (DCP), where she was responsible for all business affairs and legal matters relating to the hit television series, *So You Think You Can Dance.* In addition, she handled DCP's development deals; distribution agreements; and licenses for restaurants, live stage productions, merchandise, and online, interactive, and wireless exploitation of the library properties.

Before joining DCP, Mona spent six years at Viacom Consumer Products, the licensing division for Paramount Pictures, Spelling Television, and other companies, where she negotiated and drafted licenses of every kind from consumer products and publishing to restaurants and theme parks. She handled cutting-edge interactive, online, and wireless transactions and had primary responsibility for Paramount's stage play licensing business.

Mona graduated from UCLA School of Law after graduating with honors from Princeton University. She also completed the Executive Program at UCLA's Anderson School of Business. After law school, she joined a boutique entertainment law firm where she was responsible for their film, television, and music divisions. Then she went in-house for one of the firm's clients, Bonneville Worldwide Entertainment, as Vice President of Business Affairs.

"In addition to her legal work, she is a founding member, director, and officer of the Dizzy Feet Foundation, a non-profit charitable organization that provides scholarships to talented dance students and dance education programs to underprivileged children, and a member of the Board of Trustees of the Junior Statesmen Foundation, a non-partisan political education organization for high school students."

Profile of a Former Writer's Guild Lawyer

Grace was a senior lawyer at the Writer's Guild of America (WGA) for twenty-three years. Because she had worked there since her law school externship, she was an exception to the rule that you have to have two years of experience before the Writer's Guild will hire you. Grace attended law school in Los Angeles where she worked as an extern at the WGA during the summer after her second year. Following her externship, Grace continued to volunteer at the Guild during her third year and made herself indispensable by studying the WGA Basic Agreement and becoming an expert on the provisions of the agreement. Since the agreement did not have an index, she became the human index for it. Grace's hard work as a volunteer paid off when the Guild offered her a permanent job after she took the bar.

Grace recommends externships as a way to become familiar with the work of the organization and meet the people who will hire the lawyers when the need arises. Grace met the right people (lawyers in the department with hiring authority) during her externship and made herself a vital part of the legal department as a volunteer. She mastered a job that no one else wanted, which secured her position with the Guild.

Grace loved her work hours and conditions. Not making as much money as many of her classmates finally motivated her take an in-house position at The Walt Disney Studios. She loves her job at the Disney Channel, where her job flexibility allows her to participate in legal education. She enjoys lecturing to law school classes and at continuing legal education programs.

Profile of a Television Agent

Scott is a literary agent specializing in half-hour television comedies. (Literary agents represent scriptwriters.) He is a partner in a small boutique agency that specializes in television. Prior to joining the boutique agency, Scott was a literary agent specializing in television comedies at one of the big three talent agencies.

Scott attended law school in New York City, and while he was a student, he worked at one of the major studios as an intern. To supplement his income, Scott performed stand-up comedy. After passing the bar, Scott worked at a New York law firm that serviced the studio where he had interned. After a couple of years in practice, Scott applied for a position in the Business Affairs department of that studio. Because Scott had continued his relationships with the studio executives for whom he had worked, they let him know about the opening. For two years, Scott worked in the studio's New York office in the Business Affairs department. When he heard about an internal opening in Los Angeles in the television Business Affairs department, Scott applied for the transfer and was hired for the position. Because his superiors knew that Scott was a stand-up comic, they assigned him to the television comedy department.

Scott wanted to become more involved in the creative development of the programs. He made it a point to read the scripts for the shows under consideration in his spare time. He also made it a point to attend the internal meetings where the script was discussed, so that he could participate in the script evaluation. On weekends, he would take scripts home and write "coverage" of the scripts for evaluation by the creative executives. He enjoyed reading scripts so much that he decided he wanted to change careers and become a literary agent.

Because of his background and years in the entertainment industry, Scott was able to start at one of the big three talent agencies as an agent. The normal career path for agents begins in the mail room. After six to eighteen months in the mailroom, the next step is a position as an agent's assistant, answering the phones and performing other administrative tasks for the agent. An aspiring agent can work as an assistant for six months to two years before being promoted to the position of agent or fired. As with any job, there is no assurance that an individual employee will progress to the next level.

Scott worked at the large agency for ten years as a literary agent specializing in half-hour television sitcoms. Scott wasn't looking for another job, but a small boutique agency approached him about joining it as a partner. He accepted the offer because working at a smaller agency gave him the opportunity and freedom to develop material. Once Scott made the move, he realized how much of his time was spent dealing with the internal bureaucracy at the large agency. Scott is happy to be at the smaller, specialized agency. He expects this job to be his last job since he enjoys his work and his work environment.

CONCLUSION

Fueled by their desire to work in this television, the lawyers profiled above have strategically managed their careers in order to find a career in the industry. Like Ben, who was determined to work in the recording industry, their previous employment experiences and legal educations have helped them realize their dreams.

Chapter 7

THE ART OF REPRESENTING ARTISTS

Fine artists have lawyers, too. Not many lawyers specialize in art law, but there is an art law practice because artists need lawyers to assist them with copyrights, licensing, sales, and displays.

Most lawyers who specialize in art law work in New York City, where most major art auctions are held. They are not usually held in California because California has a law that requires the seller of a piece of art to pay the artist ten percent of the proceeds. Art auctions held in New York City avoid this "tax."

However, there are a few art lawyers spread thinly across the country. Those who practice art law generally are engaged in other related entertainment practices including intellectual property.

Mainstream entertainment lawyers do not consider "art law" as a part of entertainment law. For an example of how the entertainment industry views artists who create fine art, watch the movie *The Player*. Art law is considered a subcategory of copyright and contract law rather than entertainment law, and law students interested in this field would do well to concentrate on these subjects. Several schools offer classes in art law or law of the visual arts.

Profiles of Two Art Law Specialists

Jane has been practicing art law exclusively for over fifteen years. Jane received her Bachelor of Arts degree from a nationally ranked university in Southern California. She received her Masters of Arts degree from a nationally ranked university in Northern California. Her Master's thesis was published in an international art journal. Jane received her JD degree from the same Northern California school.

Prior to attending law school, Jane used her master's degree as an entree into the art world. She worked as the director of a contemporary art gallery for several years. She served on the national board of directors of an art gallery association and has been elected to the boards of other organizations.

Since graduating from law school, Jane has written extensively on art law and teaches as an adjunct professor at several law schools. She has offices in New York and in Los Angeles and constantly travels between the two.

Jane represents art galleries and some artists. She is active in the American Bar Association and several museum boards and societies. Jane lectures on art law regularly for continuing legal education programs and art industry organizations. Lecturing helps her to expand and develop her practice.

Jane's diverse activities allow her to practice exclusively in art law and make a comfortable living so that she can participate in the New York art market. Jane has been able to combine her avocation for art with her vocation as a lawyer.

Like Jane, Bill has been able to make art law his specialty. A partner in the tenth largest law firm in Hawaii, he began his entertainment law practice with some basic copyright work for local artists. After graduating from a law school in the Northwest, Bill moved to Hawaii and was hired by his current firm. His copyright workload increased as he set a goal to develop an intellectual property law practice.

At a gallery show, Bill met an up-and-coming artist who was just starting to get noticed outside Hawaii. Bill began to work with the artist and discovered that the artist had not registered his art with the Copyright Office and had neglected to register his service marks and trademarks. Just as the artist's work was becoming internationally recognized, Bill's firm undertook the task of protecting all of the artist's intellectual property. That kept the firm exceptionally busy. The legal work has leveled off now that the artist has moved away from Hawaii. Fortunately for the artist, Bill taught him the importance of protecting his work.

Growing an intellectual property law practice with an internationally famous client has provided Bill with interesting practice challenges. He consults a local law school professor on technical interpretations of intellectual property law, and he associates with local counsel when the artist has an out-of-state legal problem. Bill has developed an expertise in intellectual property law so that he can handle all of his client's needs. He speaks on the subject at continuing legal education seminars and regularly addresses community groups about copyright law.

With a solid intellectual property practice, Bill has sought to expand the scope of his practice to include other areas of entertainment law. The opportunity to expand came when he was referred a large copyright infringement case brought by a mainland music publishing company. The music publishing company needed local counsel to sue a Hawaiian company that was making pirate records and distributing them throughout the Hawaiian Islands. Because the Hawaiian music community is small, word of the lawsuit spread quickly. Because Bill was representing the plaintiff in the suit against a company that most of the local musicians were afraid to cross, he gained immediate recognition as a champion for the rights of artists. Since that lawsuit, Bill's music practice has grown steadily. He now represents several of the top musical acts in Hawaii. In addition, he continues to attract other entertainment industry clients who need representation in Hawaii.

Bill has been active in trying to educate the performing artist community in Hawaii because the local music community has not followed the law as carefully as it should. Bill holds seminars for artists to educate them on their rights and responsibilities under the copyright laws, and the educational seminars generate clients for his practice. Bill generally represents a new artist on a pro bono basis. The clients who "make it" always come back. Doing pro bono work for industry clients has been a successful strategy for developing his practice.

Bill has been one of the proponents of the financial incentive laws that Hawaii has passed to attract film and television projects. He regularly lobbies the state legislature and brings his clients to testify to add star power to their lobbying efforts. He is active in all aspects of the creative community, which generates clients for his firm.

Through dedication to their goals, Jane and Bill have been able to develop art law practices. While Jane travels between LA and New York, Bill has demonstrated that it is possible to live outside the major art centers of the world and develop an entertainment law practice. His experience also illustrates that one can find success in a specialty field working for artists who need legal services to protect their work.

Chapter 8
LITERATURE AND WRITERS

Scriptwriters, playwrights, and authors all have their own guilds to represent them and their profession. Each guild has a group of in-house lawyers. In addition, individual members hire lawyers to represent them along with their agents.

WRITERS GUILD OF AMERICA

Writers of scripts and screenplays for movies and television are represented by their agents and the Writers Guild of America (WGA). The WGA represents its members in disputes over credits and pay as set forth in the lengthy Minimum Basic Agreement between the WGA and the Alliance of Motion Picture and Television Producers.

Writer's credits are determined by specific guild rules negotiated to protect the writer from losing credit for his or her work. Disputes over writer's credit are handled by a panel of three writer-members of the guild who read all of the drafts of a particular script and determine, within the guild guidelines, who should receive credit for writing the script. This anonymous peer review system normally produces equitable results for all of the writers involved with a particular project.

The Basic Agreement includes minimum pay scales for writers depending on the format of the writing. There are specific amounts for treatment, scripts, and rewrites. In addition, the fees vary for half-hour television programs, one-hour television programs, and two-hour television movies. Feature films have a higher base scale for all of the types of writing involved. All network television programs and feature films released by a member studio must comply with the guild agreement whether the individual writer is a member of the guild or not.

Since the agreement calls for arbitration of all disputes, the five Los Angeles–based WGA lawyers spend the majority of their time preparing for and representing members in arbitration hearings. The WGA East in New York City has two staff lawyers who represent their members. The WGA East primarily represents television news writers while the West Coast WGA primarily represents television sitcom, drama, and feature writers.

Profile of Two WGA Lawyers

Lee is senior counsel at the headquarters of the WGA in Los Angeles. After graduating from law school in Los Angeles, he accepted a position with a labor law firm he had clerked with the summer between his second and third years of law school. He worked at the law firm for two years before accepting a position in the legal business affairs department at a motion picture and television studio in Burbank, California. He left the studio after applying for his current job, which was advertised in the trade publications.

The WGA staff lawyers generally work 9:30 a.m. to 5:30 p.m. with no weekend work. Since the standard writer's contract stipulates that the *situs* of any dispute is Los Angeles, all of the arbitrations are in Los Angeles and the lawyers generally do not travel. Lee, however, does travel occasionally to New York and Toronto to meet with the other WGA administrators to discuss and formulate policy. Because of his extra duties, he does not keep the same regular hours as the other staff lawyers. He typically works more hours than his colleagues.

WGA lawyers are compensated commensurate with their experience. Salaries are generally better than those offered by union labor firms and comparable to the salaries paid to other in-house counsel.

Two years' experience in labor law is the minimum prerequisite for employment at the WGA, according to Lee. They generally recruit labor lawyers with arbitration experience rather than entertainment lawyers, and do not look for people who are solely interested in entertainment law. The Guild has a high rate of turnover as lawyers use the position and experience as an entry into entertainment law, moving into studio positions or law firms after their work with the guild. This is a common career path recommended by industry insiders, including Lee.

Lee feels that his work experience more than his law school experience prepared him for his current position. His on-the-job training came from years at the union labor law firm and the studio.

Melissa is an associate counsel at the Writers Guild of America West. She spends the majority of her days negotiating with studio executives and in-house counsel at various production agencies regarding contractual disputes, compensation, residuals, and intellectual property issues on behalf of screen and television writers. When she is not able to reach a settlement with the studio and/or production agency, she takes the matter to arbitration, state or federal court, or files a petition with the National Labor Relations Board.

Melissa explains, "Unlike traditional litigation, entertainment labor is all about relationships. When I worked as an entertainment litigator at a big [international law] firm, relationships with opposing counsel were extremely contentious and adversarial. Opposing counsel rarely worked toward finding a resolution that was best for both parties and instead sought to win at all costs by taking the most aggressive approach possible. This approach was usually not the most cost-effective method of reaching a resolution for the client. Unlike the traditional litigation environment, which is saturated with lawyers, entertainment labor is extremely specialized and a close niche. As a result, entertainment labor lawyers often deal with the same opposing counsel on a number of matters. This creates an incentive to form more collegial relationships. Entertainment labor lawyers usually work together to achieve a settlement that is in the best interest of all parties."

Melissa interned at NBC in the music department after filling out an application online. While this position was not specifically related to law, it helped her land an internship at the Screen Actors Guild while she was in law school. Her experience at SAG helped her get a job with Katten, Muchin, Rosenman LLP in the entertainment litigation department after law school. She worked for the firm for six years and then decided to transition to an in-house position so she could "focus exclusively on entertainment matters having to do with labor and employment issues . . . . I saw an ad for an open position at the Writers Guild of America on LinkedIn, and I applied." Melissa was contacted by the Human Resources director who called her in for an interview. Following the interview, she received the offer she was hoping for.

Melissa loves her job. She says that the only drawback is that she doesn't get to travel outside Los Angeles and New York for work. Because most firms will not hire a new lawyer for their entertainment department, she recommends an internship during law school to establish some relationship in the entertainment field. "Try to get a job in a general litigation department that handles a lot of entertainment disputes, or a corporate department that often takes on overflow work from its entertainment group. After a few years, you should be in a better position to land a job specializing in entertainment law.

"If you are looking to break into the creative side of entertainment, as opposed to a financial or legal career in entertainment, expect to spend many years working your way up the ladder for little pay. The climb to the top for creative positions in entertainment is extremely competitive. You will likely need to start in the mail room or as an assistant."

DRAMATISTS GUILD

Approximately 9,000 playwrights belong to the Dramatists Guild headquartered in New York City. The Guild has two staff lawyers in its New York office who review, free of charge for guild members, production agreements for compliance with the Approved Production Contract (APC) for Broadway plays and musicals. The guild also has agreements for off-Broadway productions and smaller, local venues. These later agreements have more negotiable areas than does the APC for Broadway productions, which are referred to as first-class productions.

The APC is a non-negotiable minimum contract setting forth the compensation due the playwright and the rights of the parties involved. Unlike members of the WGA, playwrights retain ownership in the copyright. The APC is similar to a lease rather than an employment contract. Playwrights are guaranteed ten percent of the weekly box office gross and retain all movie rights. The APC varies significantly from the standard movie or television contract.

There is a shortage of knowledgeable lawyers specializing in playwright representation. The guild retains outside counsel in New York City to handle litigation and assist in contract negotiations, but beyond the few specialists in New York City, there are very few qualified practitioners. As theater moves out of New York City and into other metropolitan areas, the opportunity for a copyright or tax specialist to expand in this field should develop.

Most playwrights do not have individual representation beyond the guild because of the shortage of knowledgeable lawyers. One reason for the shortage is economic. The saying in the industry is, "You can't make a living in theater, but you can make a killing." Theater productions are so expensive that only the very successful productions recoup their costs.

Playwrights do retain counsel for merchandising representation and motion picture exploitation. There is no shortage of entertainment specialists practicing in these areas.

AUTHORS GUILD

Authors are represented by the Authors Guild and their own agents. The Authors Guild has no in-house counsel at its New York City headquarters and only retains counsel as needed. The majority of authors have agents who negotiate contracts for them; however, an author does need a lawyer to negotiate the author-agent contract.

While some literary agents are lawyers, the majority of agents are non-lawyers who negotiate contracts without the services of a lawyer. Agents will retain a lawyer to review a complex agreement on behalf of the author in special instances.

Chapter 9

EXPLORING OTHER OPTIONS IN THE FIELD OF ENTERTAINMENT LAW

The lawyers profiled make it clear that the majority of entertainment work is in New York, Los Angeles, and Nashville, but Atlanta, Chicago, Miami, and Minneapolis have enough business to support an entertainment bar. Atlanta has become a hotbed for rap, hip-hop, and R&B music. CNN, TNT, and TBS are all headquartered there. Chicago has WGN and is the backdrop for several film and television productions. Miami is the headquarters for all of the labels' Latin music divisions as well as television and film productions. Minneapolis is the home of the empire created by Prince. While Orlando used to be the boy-band capital of the world, it is still home to Disney World, Universal Studios, EA Sports, Full Sail, and an independent animation studio.

As a general rule, the majority of the lawyers practicing law in the entertainment industry are in the major media centers. While there is the need for entertainment legal work in virtually every city with an Internet connection, the depth and breadth of that work varies depending on the sophistication of the client and the size of the operation.

The "typical" entertainment lawyer working outside of one of the media centers works for a firm with a client base diverse enough to include some entertainment clients. Many entertainment specialists are also copyright specialists, labor relations lawyers, tax lawyers, litigation specialists, or corporate lawyers.

Like anyone else who needs legal services, the entertainment industry client seeks a qualified lawyer practicing in the area in which the client needs advice. Expertise is then adapted to fit the entertainment client's needs just as it is adapted to fit the needs of the lawyer's other clients. To that end, a good lawyer is a good lawyer and will attract clients (of all types) because of his or her quality work.

Since the major clients can normally afford the best lawyers, the way to become a good entertainment lawyer is to become a good lawyer in a specialty area that industry clients regularly need. As you begin to represent more and more industry clients, your expertise in the field will increase and you will be able to specialize further.

While the business is generally a closed community (you have to know someone to get a break), a good lawyer with a good reputation will eventually meet someone who will be able to use his or her expertise. If your goal is to work for an entertainment corporation, guild, or union, you will need quality law firm experience before you will be considered for an opening. Entertainment law experience is not often necessary for a corporate, guild, or union position.

The most common advice from the responding practitioners is to learn the business. A first step is reading the trade publications. If you understand the entertainment business, you can adapt your legal expertise to fit the unique situations that arise in an industry practice. The second most common advice is to do well in law school and graduate at or near the top of your class. Since the field sounds attractive to so many students and new lawyers, the supply far exceeds the demand, allowing firms to choose the most talented individuals to practice with their firms.

Profile of an Industry Heavyweight

Peter had been involved in the media and entertainment business long before deciding to go to law school. He started his career at his college radio station at Yale. After that, he worked as summer relief for operating engineers (from camera to sound mixer) for WTTG-TV (Washington, DC) and KABC-TV (Los Angeles). From there he became a television news writer for Channel 9 in Los Angeles. Peter worked as an assistant director for public relations for the Los Angeles Philharmonic/Hollywood Bowl; attended one year of UCLA's Graduate School of Theater, Film, and Television in the MFA program; and was a producer/director of industrial film for VTN in Orange County, California. When he graduated from law school, entertainment law was a logical step.

Following graduation, he joined an entertainment law firm that ultimately bore his name. After many years at the firm, he left to become of counsel to Weissmann Wolff. After that firm merged, he started his current practice. Peter is exceptionally busy. He is typically up at 6:00 a.m. to write his blog and answer emails from other time zones. He arrives at the office at around 9:00 a.m. for meetings. Peter stays at the office "until everything is relatively under control." He reports that he has had one day off, including holidays, in the past eight years.

Peter is well known in the industry and loves "helping get great films and television programs into being." He enjoys "guiding clients in transitions, providing my favorite skill set— deal and structural architecture—to companies and financiers that listen!" Peter dislikes dealing with "time sheets, collections, and clients who don't listen and expect you to fix it when what you predicted would go wrong if they didn't listen actually does."

For those wanting to get into the business, Peter recommends that you "find a focus that differentiates you from the masses of wannabe entertainment lawyers. Learn the numbers of the industry, the barriers, the myths and the role of marketing." It has been exceptionally rewarding for Peter.

Profiles of General Practitioners Who Specialize in Entertainment Law

Law firms of all sizes engage in entertainment law practice. The following profiles are illustrative of some of the general practice options available.

Delynn works at a firm in Montana. She left her job at a major studio in Los Angeles as a lawyer in the Legal and Business Affairs department to move to Montana. Delynn represents musicians, authors, producers, publishers, and Internet-based and local businesses. In addition to entertainment law, she helps clients with technology, business, immigration, and estate planning issues. She telecommutes in her representation of her entertainment clients.

Delynn grew up in Southern California. During college, she was a producer/reporter and disc jockey at her college radio station, and she worked for the head of the communications department of KTTV, a Los Angeles news station for two years. She graduated with honors, and her college work helped her get an internship at KTTV. While she was there, she "accepted a second concurrent internship as a researcher and production assistant for a children's program— *Flip*—that won an Emmy."

After that, Delynn took a job as a secretary at a small independent entertainment company in the music department. She worked her way up through the ranks to become an assistant in the legal department. She was in charge of copyright clearances and other rights clearances in addition to performing her other administrative duties. Delynn decided law school could help her move to the next level within the company so she left the company to study law.

While attending a Southern California law school, she interned at Universal Studios and Sony/Columbia TriStar. She also worked as a temporary for the legal counsel for All American Communication, *Baywatch*, and Scotti Bros. Records. After her first year in law school, Delynn went back to Scotti Bros. to work in the legal department. The company had two lawyers and several clerk/interns in the legal department. Since she was familiar with the company, Delynn was able to work on all of the interesting projects with the General Counsel.

During the second semester of her second year, Delynn took a part-time internship at the studio where she worked before she moved to Montana. She worked in the legal department as a clerk. She really enjoyed the differences and challenges of working in the feature film department. Delynn continued to work at the studio as a part-time volunteer for the remainder of her law school career.

In law school, Delynn took courses in copyright, trademark, business law, and contracts, as well as seminarsin negotiations and arbitration. With her tongue firmly planted in her cheek, she said, "The courses that helped me the most with my career were the music seminar and the entertainment law course taught by Professor Henslee."

Following the bar exam, Delynn was told by the studio that they could not hire her because she did not have any law firm experience. Since she had not worked in a law firm during law school, Delynn did not have any law firm job prospects. Her old company offered her a job to return as an administrator but not as a lawyer. Since she had worked for them as a secretary, many of the senior officers could not see her working for the company as a lawyer. Delynn was not interested in returning as a low-level administrator.

Delynn decided to start her own law firm. She started by contacting some of the bands she had worked with while at the record company. The bands referred clients to her, but most of the clients could not pay her fees. Delynn started volunteering with the California Lawyers for the Arts group. Her work with the starving artists started to pay off as many of the people she helped came back to her as clients when they had legal problems. In addition to her music clients, Delynn took clients who were fashion models. As her practice expanded, she was offered an of-counsel position with a firm interested in starting an entertainment department. Delynn moved into their downtown offices and began attracting more clients.

Delynn's dream was to work at the studio. She was not happy working as a solo lawyer, even with the support she was receiving in her new of-counsel affiliation. Her clients were not generating enough business to pay her expenses and law school loans and still provide a comfortable income. Delynn heard about an in-house legal position at a private Internet provider company, interviewed for the position, and accepted the job.

Delynn was the in-house counsel for the company as the company grew from forty employees to six hundred employees. The company began to take steps to go public and retained outside counsel for their initial public offering. Delynn's responsibilities grew dramatically. Because she had passed the bar only eighteen months earlier, she felt overwhelmed by her responsibilities, which included all of the intellectual property work the company generated as well as its employment issues and issues related to the public offering. Because the company's product was intellectual property, Delynn was forced to become an expert on Internet licensing, rights acquisition, and secondary-provider liability. The company was happy with Delynn's work, so they did not see the need to hire another lawyer to help her. After discussing her workload and responsibilities, the company president decided to offer Delynn the job of general counsel and let her staff the legal department. Delynn was offered a substantial raise and a stock option.

While Delynn was thinking about the offer, the studio called and offered Delynn an entry-level job as a legal assistant in the Legal and Business Affairs department. The department's philosophy was to hire lawyers to work as legal assistants for very low pay. When a position opened in the department, one of the lawyers who was working as a legal assistant would be asked to fill the position since that person was familiar with the department.

Delynn was torn. She had two offers: an offer to become the general counsel of an up-and-coming Internet company or an offer to work as a legal assistant at the studio where she had always dreamed of working. She took the studio position and says she does not regret the move. Even though she took a cut in pay and status, she enjoyed her work and the benefits of working at a studio. Delynn was offered a job as a lawyer shortly after joining the department as a legal assistant. It was not easy, but by keeping up her contacts at the studio and working to get the legal background the studio needed, she finally got the job she had wanted since law school.

After a short time at the studio, she left the studio to move to Montana. Her experience with the Internet service provider still generates clients for her practice. She enjoys "being a part of the business and creative process for her clients and helping them protect their interests." She says, "With immigration matters, I enjoy helping clients realize their dream of becoming a United States citizen." She does not enjoy "the administrative aspects of running a solo practice." Time tracking, billing, and self-promotion are a necessary part of the job, but not personally rewarding.

For those interested in getting into the business, Delynn says, "Be persistent. Don't get too caught up in the celebrity. Treat the deals as business first. Don't take the business too personally; always be real and honest in your dealings. You will only be as strong as your reputation, so guard it well, and earn one worthy of respect."

Henry is a partner in an international law firm with about six hundred lawyers nationwide. He is a member of the firm's sixteen-person entertainment department in Los Angeles. As the senior partner in the entertainment department, he has become a specialist, but he still practices in the areas of real estate and corporate law.

His clients include small businesses, producers, directors, talent, insurance companies, and financial institutions. He negotiates and drafts agreements, which range from material acquisition to talent buying to structuring the investment participation for financing. Henry deals with talent agents, as well as the business affairs and legal departments at the studios, assisting them in structuring complex agreements.

Henry graduated from a law school in Washington, DC, and began work for his present firm in their New York office thirty-four years ago. He was one of the partners who moved to Los Angeles to open the firm's expansion office.

Henry makes a substantial income as a partner, but he must work long hours and at least one weekend day on a regular basis. His clients demand that he be available at their convenience, and they are willing to pay for that privilege. The hours are demanding, but the work is both challenging and personally rewarding.

Since he is a transactional lawyer, the majority of his time is spent in meetings either on the phone or in person. He spends the remainder of his time reviewing documents prepared by his associates for his clients.

Fred: Not all entertainment lawyers practice in Los Angeles or New York. Fred, for example, is a partner in an eighty-person firm in Chicago that has a three-member entertainment department. The department deals mainly with contract negotiation, litigation, advertising clearance, and FCC Act business. Their clients include industrial corporations, networks and studios, advertising agencies, and talent.

After graduating from an Ivy League law school, Fred worked in New York for one year at a large law firm before moving to Chicago. As a registered patent lawyer he was assigned to an entertainment-related client at his first Chicago firm. His background in the protection of intellectual property rights was helpful when he was called on to learn copyright law. His practice has grown since that assignment.

Since Fred currently is a senior partner, he is comfortably compensated. While his work is concentrated in Chicago, he frequently is required to travel to Los Angeles or New York, and occasionally Washington, DC. His workday requires many hours at the office, and he normally works six days a week.

Mike, like Fred, works long hours and at least one weekend day for his firm in Salt Lake City. The firm, which has thirty-two lawyers, is engaged in a general civil practice. Mike is developing the firm's entertainment practice and has attracted clients by becoming involved in the local entertainment community. From his work in employment relations, he began representing the local symphony musicians. This work led to referrals by the musicians and he now has a growing list of musician clients. His work normally includes negotiating and drafting contracts and copyright advice.

Mike began working for his current firm after graduation from a Midwestern law school. Now a partner, he is competitively compensated. While the other partners have allowed him to develop an entertainment practice, they have required that he maintain a minimum billable hour schedule doing general civil work.

Jack is a lawyer in St. Paul with a passion for film. After graduating from law school, he began a production company that filmed commercials and educational and industrial films. After two years of producing films, Jack founded a law firm. His client base grew from his work in the entertainment industry and includes performing and recording musicians, textbook authors, and producers of commercial and industrial media. His two-person firm practices in the areas of family law, real estate, and employment discrimination as well as entertainment law.

Jack has been working to establish his firm in the past five years and he has not had much time off. With only two lawyers in his firm, he is not afforded the luxury of client cultivation without billable hours. As his practice grows, he expects to be able to hire more lawyers and take some time off.

Josh began his firm career at the Beverly Hills firm of Freund & Brackly in the entertainment and intellectual property litigation department after clerking for the Chief Justice of the California Supreme Court. Preferring to focus on transactional work, he formed his own firm with clients such as Cheech & Chong, Jaleel White (Urkel from *Family Matters*), and the production companies for Method Man and R. Kelly. He has negotiated deals with "The Weinstein Company, MTV, E! Channel, VH1, Interscope, and Def Jam, to name a few." Josh focuses on representing talent for film, music, new media, and television. He earned a MBA in addition to his JD, and says that his business education is as useful as his legal education. He recommends both degrees for someone looking for an edge to break into the entertainment business.

As illustrated by the previous profiles, the majority of practicing entertainment lawyers begin their practice in a related field and develop an entertainment practice as they become established.

Some of the larger firms in Los Angeles and New York hire associates specifically for their entertainment departments. But these firms tend to hire only top students from top law schools across the nation, thus limiting this opportunity to a select few.

Breaking into entertainment law requires quality work both in school and in practice. Unless you already know someone, your best bet for gaining entry to this field is to develop contacts in the industry through professional activities in the legal or entertainment field. Attendance at CLE programs is a great way to meet entertainment industry professionals.

NON-LEGAL CAREERS

There are a number of non-legal careers in the entertainment field where lawyers who are not interested in practicing law may find work. Alternatives to the practice of law in the entertainment field include talent management, talent bookings or promotions, syndication sales, and industry management. There are also lawyers who became "talent" as actors, singers, writers, producers, and directors.

If you think you have what it takes to make a living as an entertainer, then you should pursue your interests. Keep in mind, however, that success requires total dedication. Talent buyers like to see a total commitment to a career in the industry before they take a chance on someone, spend a lot of money to promote his or her career, and make the individual or group "a star." Most "overnight" discoveries are people or groups who have been working in the industry for years trying to get a break.

Many of the top executives at the networks and studios also have legal training. At some point in their careers, they made the shift from law practice to management, so they could climb out of the legal department into upper management. An understanding of the creative process and an eye for talent and great material are required to reach the top of a studio or entertainment company. Lawyers unwilling to make the transition from law will top out in the legal department. Management skills, including expertise in business and finance, are a prerequisite for the best non-legal industry jobs.

SALES

Some lawyers leave the practice of law to pursue a sales career, often in real estate development and sales or investment banking. Lawyers interested in entertainment can try industry sales or merchandising with an eye to moving up the management ladder.

Profile of a Born Salesman

Steve's profile is illustrative. His father has been in the entertainment industry for over twenty years and Steve, who shares this interest, selected a West Coast law school that had an entertainment curriculum. Steve's father promoted some of the biggest prize fights in the late 1970's and 1980's. Sales and promotions are in Steve's blood. After graduation from law school, Steve began work at a major talent agency as an agent trainee for a year before he heard about an opening in the legal department of an industry conglomerate.

Once he began working for the conglomerate, he regularly reviewed the internal job placement memos. Within a year, he transferred from his position in the legal department to a position in the sales department. The sales job required Steve to move to the Midwest. He took the transfer so he could establish himself in sales with the goal of transferring back to the corporate headquarters in Los Angeles.

After transferring back to Los Angeles, Steve took an opportunity to join an independent production company as their general counsel. The company specialized in syndicated television programming. From that position, he became general counsel at a communications company that wanted his expertise to help the company use its phone sex and psychic networks to develop cable television programming, which could benefit from the company's national telephone service. After working at that company for two years, Steve moved to a major studio to develop original sporting events for television. Steve then opened his own media consulting company so that he could continue to work with many of his previous employers on an independent basis. Steve is currently a partner in a firm that specializes in independent film sales, both domestically and abroad. He travels to the major film festivals to buy and sell rights to his client's films.

PROMOTIONS AND TALENT BOOKING

Legal training can be helpful for someone interested in becoming a booking agent or promoter. However, a law degree is certainly not a necessary job prerequisite since the vast majority of agents and promoters are not lawyers. Someone interested in a job as an agent or a promoter would be better served working in the industry establishing contacts rather than going to law school.

That being said, a substantial number of agents at the major talent agencies have law degrees. Positions at the agencies are extremely competitive. As mentioned previously, wannabe agents typically start in the mailroom of an agency. It is not unusual to find a number of lawyers and MBAs from well regarded schools working in the mailroom for an opportunity to move to an assistant's desk and then to become an agent. A law degree is an asset to an agent who makes a living negotiating contracts for clients.

Profile of an Agent on the Fast Track

Ed was a recent law school graduate who used his family connections to get a job in the mailroom at one of the top agencies in Los Angeles. Every night, Ed would take home scripts to read so that he could discuss them with the agents as he delivered their mail. Ed had a talent for spotting good writing, which the agents noticed. After only six months in the mailroom, Ed was moved to an assistant's desk. The normal stay in the mailroom is eighteen to twenty-four months. Within a year, Ed was promoted to agent. He was fast-tracked because he had a keen eye for good writing and he was aggressive, taking the initiative to read scripts and talk about them with the agent he thought was most likely to be interested in the material. Ed used his time in the mailroom to learn the likes and dislikes of the agents in the firm and used that information to present material tailored to each agent's likes. His talent was noticed and he was rewarded. Ed spent a lot of off-duty time reading so that he could impress the right people. His hard work paid off. He is now a partner in the agency.

TALENT MANAGEMENT

Talent management is an area where a legal education can be beneficial. Talent managers regularly review and negotiate contracts on behalf of their clients. Again, while a law degree is not a prerequisite for the job, many individuals seeking management feel more comfortable with the qualifications and abilities of a law-educated manager.

Profile of a Talent Manager

Steven's profile is a good example. He moved from Miami, where he was a partner in a music production company, to Los Angeles to attend a law school with an entertainment law program.

While in law school, he handled the bookings west of the Mississippi for the Miami company's major dance music act. Since the group had two top-ten dance tunes (on the *Billboard* charts), it was easy to get his phone calls returned.

On occasion, he would spend time on the road with the group acting as their road manager. After graduating from law school and passing the California Bar, he began his own law practice while he continued to book the group. His association with the national touring act introduced him to a number of record company executives and promoters. His goal was to become a full-time manager, so he did not have to rely on legal work or bookings.

Steven's break came two years later when he ran into a friend he had not seen since their bar review class. They started talking, and as it turned out, the friend, also a lawyer involved in talent management, was looking to associate with someone to take over his duties as a personal manager so that he could spend more time with his law practice.

With the client's permission, Steven took over the friend's personal representation of the recording artist from a major label, and he has been able to devote his entire career to developing her act. Once he associated with her, he was in demand as a talent manager. His success with her has allowed him to become very selective in his choice of clients.

Steven gets phone calls at all hours of the night and works weekends, days, and nights, but he loves his work. He knows that his income is dependent on his clients' income, so he works hard to ensure that they do everything they can to further their careers and maximize earnings. He is rarely able to take time off, but he can go out on the road with one of his acts when he needs a break in his non-routine. Steven says his most difficult problem is finding enough hours in the day to complete his work.

While non-legal entertainment careers do not require a law degree, and the majority of the people currently in those positions are not legally trained, the educational background coupled with bar passage can give a lawyer an advantage over non-lawyer colleagues. More lawyers are moving into both industry management and talent management as alternatives to the practice of law.

REAL ESTATE

Warner Bros. beat all of the studios in the retail market by opening merchandise outlets in shopping malls across the country. These studio stores have been so successful that Disney followed Warner Bros. Disney is escalating the stakes by developing theme malls based on their franchise characters and theme parks. The theme mall experiment has been successfully test-marketed and should spread across the country as quickly as Disney can develop them. Warner Bros. will likely follow.

Look for the other studios to follow the lead of Warner Bros. and Disney. All of the studios rely on merchandise revenue from their pictures to supplement a film's gross income. Opening theme malls is the next logical step in the expansion of the studio's products. Universal Studios and MGM both have theme parks that they can use as patterns for theme malls.

Combining merchandising with real estate development will create new revenue streams for the studios by providing greater access to their products. New feature films and television shows can be introduced at the mall stores with trailers and posters. Also, the theme malls serve as advertisements for the theme parks and attract new customers to the theme parks.

Chapter 10
CAREER CHARACTERISTICS

The profiles have already provided some ideas about the lifestyles of those who choose entertainment law. This chapter will explore further the demands and rewards of this field.

LOCATION AND TRAVEL

As indicated by the lawyers profiled, entertainment lawyers tend to be clustered in New York City and Los Angeles, with a few entertainment lawyers in every other city in the nation. Nashville, Chicago, Atlanta, and Miami have growing entertainment bars.

The majority of the lawyers surveyed for this book, even those who do not live in Los Angeles or New York City, recommended admission to one or both of those two state bars since the two cities serve as headquarters for the industry. California does not have reciprocity with any other states, so you will have to sit for the California Bar if you want to practice there. New York has limited reciprocity with some states. Contact the New York State Bar Examiners for more information on their reciprocity requirements.

Since one-sixth of the nation's lawyers are members of the California Bar, the state has a tremendous supply of interested and qualified lawyers. Seventy percent of those California lawyers practice in southern California. The second largest lawyer population in the United States is in New York State.

There is no current or projected future shortage of available lawyers interested in practicing entertainment law. The supply in these two states is predicted to exceed the demand for many years into the twenty-first century. That does not mean that you cannot break into the industry; it just means that you are going to have to plan your entry and be patient as you develop expertise in one or more of the substantive areas of law commonly practiced in the industry.

A lawyer interested in developing an entertainment practice in a city outside the two entertainment hubs should approach it as he or she would approach the development of any other specialty practice. The majority of questionnaire respondents reported that an entertainment law practice develops over time after a lot of hard work at refining legal skills and developing industry contacts.

The bulk of travel in the entertainment industry is between New York City and Los Angeles with occasional trips to Nashville and Washington, DC. While most of the responding lawyers outside of these cities indicated that their practices were restricted to their home base and the surrounding areas, the New York City and Los Angeles lawyers tend to travel more and have more international clients.

THE WORLD BECKONS

Many American lawyers are interested in an entertainment law practice in Europe, Asia, and South America. One member of an international law firm, describing the opportunities in Europe, explained that a significant number of large American corporations located throughout Europe are engaged in the entertainment business or have an interest in the industry.

While some of these corporations have American staff lawyers in their European offices, the practice emphasis is more along the lines "of international law, taxation, trade and business formation, and acquisition rather than 'pure' entertainment law. In addition to the corporations, there are several American law firms with branch offices in Europe employing both American and European lawyers. Of these law firms, none are solely engaged in an entertainment practice in either the United States or Europe. Several of these firms do have entertainment departments, however."

Another group of American lawyers is engaged in small partnerships or solo practices advising local clients on United States laws and assisting American lawyers associating with local counsel. These lawyers act as legal consultants rather than lawyers engaged in the active representation of a client.

Since it is extremely difficult for an American lawyer to qualify as an English solicitor, English firms are reluctant to hire American lawyers as associates on a traditional partnership track. English and other European firms with a great deal of business in the United States hire American lawyers to handle business here.

The opportunities for an American lawyer interested in establishing a practice or associating with a European firm specializing in entertainment law are limited. U.S. corporations and large law firms tend to rotate staff lawyers from their home offices to a European branch office for a specific number of years or to work on a special project. These special assignments require an established expertise in the specialty area needed by the European branch.

One opportunity for an American lawyer seems to be establishing a practice in the European country, but this is not a viable option for a recent law school graduate. Entrepreneurial entertainment lawyers are retained by local entertainment companies and talent. Often the association will be more for personal or business representation (such as personal management for talent) rather than as a legal counsel. Europeans tend to be very territorial and resent competition from relocated American lawyers. Consequently, most countries do not make it easy for Americans to establish a local law practice.

China and India have burgeoning film industries. In an effort to support local films, many countries have limited the number of foreign (from the United States) films that can be shown in that country. Entertainment corporations have partnered with local companies to develop products that qualify to be shown in the home country and are interesting enough for a U. S. release. Law firms have opened foreign offices and partnered with local lawyers to help both foreign and domestic companies survive overseas. Most of the merchandise sold at theme parks in the United States is made overseas, requiring local counsel to comply with local regulations and coordinate the transportation of the merchandise to the United States.

With the Olympics and the World Cup visiting Brazil, cross-cultural entertainment opportunities will continue to expand. A knowledge of Portuguese for Brazil, and Spanish for the rest of the Central and South American countries, is required for anyone interested in doing business in the area. Miami is currently the United States hub for American companies doing business in South and Central America.

While local firms rarely hire American lawyers, when they need to associate with American counsel, they normally contact an established law firm that has expertise in the required area of law and that is located in the city where the problem or opportunity exists. There is resistance to hiring an American lawyer unless that lawyer also is licensed to practice in the local jurisdiction. The best opportunity for an American who desires to practice and travel in Europe is to associate with an American law firm or corporation with branch offices or subsidiaries in Europe, Asia, or South America, or with several foreign clients. After establishing a broad base of contacts and a reputation for quality expertise in the field, a lawyer who wishes to leave his or her current firm to establish or associate with a foreign firm will find a simpler job transition. Knowledge of the local language is a critical skill for employment overseas. Unless there is an entrepreneurial business in addition to the practice, the lawyer should expect earnings that are significantly lower than someone with a similar position in an American firm.

COMPENSATION AND BENEFITS

The amount of compensation for entertainment lawyers in the United States varies with the size of the law firm, location, and number of years in practice. Starting salaries are equivalent to the starting salaries of lawyers engaged in other types of transactional law practice. Questionnaire respondents reported that practitioners with five to ten years of practice have salaries that range from $30,000 to $250,000 a year. Lawyers with ten or more years of practice reported annual incomes between $75,000 and $1,000,000.

Aside from the regular health and retirement benefits offered by corporations and law firms, in-house corporate lawyers are often granted stock options and performance bonuses. Some corporations offer company cars, country club memberships, and paid continuing legal education opportunities. In-house corporate lawyers normally work fewer hours for less compensation at the top end of the salary range than do their counterparts in private practice. Beginning and mid-range salaries tend to be competitive.

Depending on the clients, a lawyer may be offered the opportunity to attend opening functions, concerts, award ceremonies, and parties. In addition to the social benefits, a lawyer may be invited to participate as an investor or partner in an entertainment venture. Production and investment opportunities present the lawyer with ethical problems, which should be fully investigated and disclosed to the other parties before the lawyer agrees to participate. Participating as a partner presents different ethical considerations than does contingent fee representation.

LIFESTYLES

Lawyers' lifestyles tend to be similar regardless of the specialty area practiced. Variations related to location are more common than variations based on the type of practice. While entertainment lawyers do travel and have the opportunity to attend entertainment-related social events, the long work hours with weekends in the office is the same as in any specialty.

In-house corporate lawyers often choose that career path because of the lifestyle. While regular hours with weekends off used to be the norm, in today's competitive market, in-house lawyers are spending as much time on the job as their counterparts in firms. Corporate travel has been reduced since companies can videoconference when necessary. Corporate lawyers usually receive the additional benefit of stock options designed to draw qualified practitioners away from private practice and into a corporate law department. Because of the slightly lower compensation, corporations use these additional benefits to recruit lawyers.

Lawyers who have close ties with "talent" can expect regular interruptions on weekends and evenings. Also, lawyers with foreign clients often get calls at irregular hours due to the time zone differences.

While there are special attractions in the field of entertainment law, the day-to-day tasks of a typical entertainment lawyer requires long hours just like any other specialized area of law.

PERSONALITY TYPES

Entertainment lawyers tend to be passionate, aggressive, intelligent, motivated individuals. They are people who will negotiate the definition of a word until both parties can live with the definition. They are detail-oriented people able to read pages of boilerplate language to make sure that the contract gives their client all of the rights negotiated. They are people with a passion for their media who will work on a project under strict deadlines. They are aggressive advocates for their client's point-of-view and who know the parameters of the deal that depend on the relative industry clout of the parties involved. They are competent lawyers with a background in a specialty area of the substantive law. *Hit and Run*, by Nancy Griffin and Kim Masters, provides an unflattering account of how Jon Peters and Peter Guber ascended by sheer force of personality from film packagers to corporate executives to run Sony Pictures. The book is entertaining as well as informative.

Depending on the media, the dress code varies. Studio lawyers wear expensive suits while music lawyers generally wear blue jeans and button down shirts. Lawyers who work in firms adhere to their firm dress code, which is generally dictated by their clients. All of the lawyers drive nice cars to give their clients the impression that the lawyers are successful.

Many entertainment lawyers spend their time during business hours on the phone. They review contracts and perform their other duties after regular business hours. You must enjoy talking on the phone and have a professional telephone presence to be successful in the entertainment business.

Socializing at breakfast, lunch, and dinner meetings is another important skill required for client development and career advancement. Entertainment clients require a great deal of personal attention in the form of phone and face-to-face contact. Social skills are essential for the lawyer to function as a part of the entertainment social scene. Socially inept introverts must advance their skills if they want to fulfill the requirements of a successful entertainment lawyer.

Chapter 11

CAREER CHANGES

Since entertainment law is an amalgamation of copyright, labor, tax, contract, and corporate law employing both negotiators and litigators, lawyers wishing to change specialty fields can easily move from entertainment law into another practice area using the same skills. Moving into a non-legal career either within the entertainment field or outside the industry also is a viable transition. The personal skills required to deal with industry clients prepare a practitioner to adapt to meet a client's diverse needs.

Another alternative to practicing entertainment law is to teach the subject at a law school. Because law schools look for professors with some practice experience, lawyers with expertise in the underlying areas of law that entertainment law comprises have both the practical skills and knowledge to teach in a law school.

Tenure-track law teaching is notoriously competitive, however, and experienced practitioners who think they might like to teach are well advised to set their sights on part-time adjunct faculty positions initially. Exceptions may occur in cases where the individual has an outstanding academic record, or has written and published extensively while in practice. Academic publications are required by most schools looking to add faculty. There are geographical

119

constraints imposed by teaching in this field because even though there are over two hundred ABA accredited law schools, they are thinly-distributed across much of the United States. Clusters of law schools—and teaching jobs—may be found only in the metropolitan areas of New York City, Boston, Chicago, Houston, Miami, San Francisco, and Los Angeles.

Consulting options range from testifying as an expert witness to providing strategy and advice to one of the parties in a litigated matter. Other practitioners or faculty members have designed and provided services such as continuing legal education programs to the practicing bar. In fact, there are as many options for the consultant as an imaginative individual can package and market. Both lawyers and law professors engage in consulting work. Serving as a consultant is an option as a career alternative or a means to supplement income.

Another option is arbitrating disputes. The American Arbitration Association refers arbitrators to parties needing to settle a dispute. The disputing parties might find a noted practitioner the best choice to serve as an impartial arbitrator. Of course, having a reputation in the field could eliminate you from consideration if both parties are familiar with your work and viewpoint.

Changing careers is possible, but it can be challenging. As law firms continue to contract, law jobs become more and more competitive. As far as skills are concerned, entertainment lawyers possess the same basic legal skills as their colleagues in other fields. As one lawyer pointed out, "For the most part, we are transactional lawyers. As such, it should not be difficult to change specialties."

Interestingly, the one career change most respondents were not willing to make was retirement. The most frequent response to the question pertaining to retirement was, "What's that?"

Entertainment lawyers, like most other specialty lawyers, see their work in the profession as their life's work. They enjoy being a part of the creative process that results in a tangible product experienced by the masses. For these highly motivated workaholics, retirement is not a goal. Being able to practice effectively for as long as possible is the goal.

Chapter 12
ADVICE TO STUDENTS

All of the lawyers who participated in the interviews conducted for this book had advice for those currently in school and considering a career in entertainment law. They included recommendations on academic background, both in undergraduate and law school, certification, and work experience.

RECOMMENDED ACADEMIC BACKGROUND

No single undergraduate major emerges as most recommended for a career as an entertainment lawyer. Undergraduate degrees in English literature, creative writing, dance, music, theater, film, and art all provide a background in each of these media. Business degrees with an emphasis in tax or management are outstanding credentials for most specialty areas of the law. A master's degree in business administration or a credential as a Certified Public Accountant is very helpful since the entertainment industry is a business with huge amounts of money at stake. The majority of the respondents, regardless of their training, indicated that a tax background was helpful, if not essential, for many industry positions. Psychology and sociology were also listed as helpful for anyone interested in dealing directly with "talent."

Several respondents obtained master degrees in a related field. While there is no clear indication that post-graduate academic work is essential, those listing master's degrees said they benefited both from the knowledge and the contacts.

All respondents agree that a strong academic performance in law school is helpful. Participation on law review, moot court, and the ABA Law Student Divisions' Client Counseling Competition and Negotiation Competition were highly recommended. The ABA Forum Committee on the Entertainment and Sports Industries welcomes students and provides opportunities for students to meet industry lawyers. Many respondents indicated that industry related clinical experiences combined with active participation in the programs of their school's entertainment law society were beneficial. Many states have entertainment law sections with opportunities for students to participate in programs and social events with local entertainment lawyers.

Recommended courses include: contracts, labor relations, worker's compensation, U.C.C., copyright and/or intellectual property, trademark, business formation, tax (personal, corporate, and partnership), entertainment, negotiations, family law, trusts, immigration law, agency, antitrust, and professional responsibility. Courses on international copyright law and international business will become essential as the entertainment industry continues its expansion as a global industry. In addition to the basics listed above, some schools have developed seminars on special problems in the law as it relates to the areas of film, music, and television. Specialty seminars give the student an opportunity to understand the business and the law as it relates to the specialty area.

Several schools offer certificates and LL.M.s in entertainment law and intellectual property. Check with the school's placement office to find out if the program has had success placing their graduates in a position in entertainment. The additional credential should separate you from the rest of the resumes that the employer receives. As always, top grades will create greater opportunities.

Internships with the legal department in a studio or industry company can prove invaluable to the student. The job allows the student to work for a company and experience the type of work a lawyer does in an entertainment legal department. While the companies generally do not hire their interns right out of law school, they do help industrious interns find work in the entertainment industry. The contacts you establish at an internship can be very helpful throughout your career in the entertainment industry.

As is true in most areas of practice, academic training alone does not prepare beginning lawyers to meet every problem a client will present. Competence will come with experience. On-the-job training is the most prevalent training method employed in the profession.

CERTIFICATION REQUIREMENTS

Bar passage is the logical professional step following graduation, and all respondents ranked membership in either the California or the New York State bars or both as helpful if not essential. All California and New York lawyers consider membership in their respective state bars as essential and highly recommend that an entertainment practitioner be licensed in both states. Lawyers living elsewhere recognize the importance of these states to the industry and recommend California or New York bar membership as desirable and important for a growing practice. Even those who responded that their own practice is regional and that membership in the state bar is sufficient reported that being a member of the California Bar would be helpful in drawing clients.

Neither New York nor California certifies entertainment specialists. Most states that certify specialists apparently do not see the practice as large enough to warrant a specialty certification. Several states certify specialists in intellectual property. Those interested in the field should check the local state bar for further information on specialty certifications.

RECOMMENDED WORK EXPERIENCE

Since the number one recommendation by the survey respondents is to understand the business side of the industry, practitioners recommend that future entertainment lawyers gain some industry-related experience.

Many respondents were entertainers who went to law school. Several recommend work as a booking agent or as talent management as an introduction to the industry. Work at a school radio station or as a concert promoter is suggested. Basically, any industry-related job that can provide insight into the business of entertainment is recommended.

Because supply exceeds demand, those interested in entertainment law careers would do well to build a strong track record of academic performance while in school and gain all the industry-related experience they can over the summer months or during other times.

Chapter 13
GETTING INTO ENTERTAINMENT

The majority of the questionnaire respondents began their legal careers practicing in a specialty substantive area of the law that is a part of an entertainment practice. Their practices generally evolved into an entertainment practice through industry clients seeking specific legal expertise. After the respondents demonstrated their quality legal representation, their clients began to retain them on other matters outside the initial specialty field. Many entertainment firms merely evolved their practice to meet the needs of their clients.

As in any industry, word spreads quickly about both qualified and unqualified lawyers. Clients who find a qualified lawyer will tell their friends in the industry who will also seek to retain that lawyer. A practice grows through quality representation.

Some of the younger lawyers who attempted to begin their practices representing industry clients found that they had to take additional clients just to pay the bills. Quality representation in related matters is the method they used to attract entertainment clients requiring their specific expertise. Establishing any type of profitable law practice is difficult, but entertainment clients will usually give a new lawyer a chance if they need representation in a related field.

A few large firms in Los Angeles and New York City now hire lawyers specifically for their entertainment departments. But the majority hire and train associates in a related field and allow the best to transfer into the entertainment department.

Solo practitioners must also establish a reputation for quality representation. Unless you know someone in the industry who is willing to give you an opportunity, it will take time to develop a profitable entertainment practice. If you can afford to work for a legal clinic that provides service to entertainment clients who are unable to hire expensive lawyers, you can establish a reputation for quality representation and create relationships with individuals who may become rich and famous. Hopefully, they will take you along with them on their way to the top.

For many recent graduates, class rank determines the type and quality of opportunities available in law firms. Top students usually get their choices of law firms and specialty departments. As you move further away from number one in the class, the opportunities become fewer, and specialty selections disappear.

For practitioners wishing to evolve their practice into the entertainment field, it is important to develop expertise in a related specialty area to facilitate the transition. For experienced lawyers, lateral law firm transfers become available with the development of expertise. Corporate opportunities are also available to experienced practitioners. Experience and a reputation for quality are the two characteristics needed to develop a successful entertainment industry specialty practice. Unless you are related to an industry mogul, practice development will take time and dedicated work.

LOOKING FOR WORK

Any job search should begin with an organized plan. To formulate an informed job search strategy you should consult *The Legal Career Guide: From Law Student to Lawyer* by Gary Munneke and Ellen

Wayne, published by the American Bar Association as part of its Career Series. The book is an insightful career-planning manual designed to help the applicant focus a job search. Several other general career-planning manuals are listed for your information in Appendix D.

Completing the self-evaluation exercises can assist in preparing an effective resume and cover letter. By highlighting your strengths, a resume could result in an interview that helps the employer find out more about the personal qualities that make you compatible with the firm. Entertainment law firms will not review a resume or cover letter from someone seeking to be an "entertainment lawyer." Firms are looking for people who want to practice a substantive area of law as a specialist. Candidates with no law firm experience are not taken seriously when law firms are reviewing applications. Summer work in a law firm is critical for securing a law firm position. As mentioned previously, industry internships are helpful for establishing contacts, but you will most likely need law firm experience to enhance your chances of landing a position in a law firm.

Students interested in a position with an entertainment law firm after graduation should first consult their law school career services office for assistance preparing their resume. The career counselors may also provide the student with a list of employers offering an entertainment specialization who interview on campus. Your career counselor can also put you in contact with alumni practitioners who can offer further advice on job opportunities and effective job search methods.

As mentioned, good grades, a high class rank, and participation on law review are the best initial stepping stones to a specialty career in the field of your choice. Absent those qualifications, a student should seek a position in which he or she will be able to master a related specialty to evolve a practice into an entertainment specialty practice.

ADVICE FOR THOSE ALREADY PRACTICING

Current practitioners should begin their search process by preparing a resume that highlights the specialty qualifications acquired over their years of practice. A lateral move from your current firm to a firm involved in an entertainment practice is a step toward the goal of an entertainment practice. The trade magazines list opportunities for lawyers on a regular basis. Your current practice should prepare you to step into the entertainment position with little or no additional training.

If you decide that it would be difficult or impossible to develop a practice in your current situation, a new firm may provide the opportunity you seek. This lateral move will likely not be directly into the entertainment department at the new firm. More often, it will be into the specialty department where you already have experience. The opportunity to work with the entertainment department lawyers will arise later. After establishing contact with the department, an internal move should not be difficult when a need arises for someone with your expertise.

Headhunters, or legal placement firms, can be very helpful in your job search because large firms and corporations hire placement firms when they are recruiting for a specific skill set or background. Because placement firms work for the employer, not the candidate, the experience can also be discouraging. Normally only large law firms can afford the placement fees, so the applicant must have credentials acceptable to those firms. It never hurts to seek a headhunter's advice before you begin your search, however. Even if the headhunter cannot place you, he or she can point you in the right direction.

An alternative to a lateral move is to break away from your current firm and establish a solo practice. Working alone will give you the freedom to develop your practice in the entertainment field. Before beginning a solo career, you should read *How to Start and*

Build a Law Practice by Jay Foonberg, published by the American Bar Association. Another option is to move from private practice into an in-house corporate, guild, or union practice. Most corporate, guild, and union legal departments engaged in the entertainment industry seek practicing lawyers with two to five years experience in a specific related specialty (FCC, labor relations, tax, litigation, intellectual property, mergers and acquisitions, etc.). Local legal newspapers, trade publications, and *The Wall Street Journal* are sources of information about these positions.

Developing a network of industry contacts is the best way to help yourself find a job in your field of interest. Attending CLEs and the ABA's Forum Committee on Entertainment and Sports Law meetings are an outstanding source for contacts in the entertainment industry. LinkedIn is another way of developing contacts. By attending industry related fundraisers, you can meet successful entertainment executives who may be able to help you find a position in the future. Subtle self-promotion will go a long way in your quest for an entertainment-related position.

OPPORTUNITIES FOR WOMEN AND MINORITIES

The majority of the respondents indicated that women and minorities do not face any special barriers in this field. Like anyone else, however, their entry into the field will be preceded by the questions: *How well did you do in school? What school did you attend?* and *Who do you know?*

Women and minorities are now working at the highest levels in the entertainment industry. While they are not as well represented in the top positions as white males, many are actively involved in entertainment practices and are becoming established as movers and shakers. Women are well represented on the creative side of the business as artists, writers, directors, and producers. Both legal and non-legal opportunities for women and minorities should continue to grow as the industry evolves to reflect the diversity of its audience.

WHO YOU KNOW COUNTS

The practice of law is a "who you know" profession. To make partner in a law firm, you have to attract clients and bring business to the firm. It does not matter what type of law you practice; you must be able to attract clients to have a successful practice.

Entertainment is also a relationships business. The importance of making contacts in this field cannot be overemphasized. Word-of-mouth in the industry is probably the primary source for job information.

To take advantage of this word-of-mouth networking in the industry, consult other lawyers in the field. Informational interviews are a good way to open a door. Asking someone to talk about himself or herself without asking for a job is a great way to get to know someone. They will be able to introduce you to the right people so that when an opening develops, you will be considered. Remember, in this business, it can be as important to know the right people as it is to possess the skill needed for the position.

It is possible to develop connections through bar association participation and community activities. Attendance at industry-related continuing education programs can help you meet the right people. Social contacts established at general bar-related activities let you know about local activities where you can continue to meet the industry people who can help your career.

Participation as a CLE speaker is helpful in establishing yourself in any field. Writing a bar journal article helps spread the word that you have valuable expertise. Attending seminars and asking intelligent questions (yes, despite what you may have heard, there is such a thing as a stupid question) can help you start a relationship with one or more of the speakers. Attending bar meetings and conventions is another good way to meet lawyers who might be able to help you in the future.

Supporting the arts locally is another way to meet future clients. Participating on local boards will help promote you to the creative community. Supporting the arts at your local college or university will expose you to potential future clients. You need to be creative in your cultivation of contacts as you expand your book of business or meet your future employer.

Chapter 14
WHAT THE FUTURE HOLDS

The Internet has changed the way we view and listen to our media. Record labels now participate in all of the artist's income streams because album sales no longer provide the income that the label needs to maintain its old models. Record companies have had to force "360" contracts on artists to remain viable. iTunes, YouTube, Internet radio, and streaming services have created a singles market further eroding album sales. Gone are the days when a record company would sign large numbers of marginally talented groups, give them a big recording budget, send them to the studio, and then never release their music to limit the record company's losses on the signing. Now the companies are more selective. As mentioned, anyone with a computer can record and post music on the Internet.

Television shows are now streamed over the Internet, and clips can be viewed on YouTube. Specialty channels have cannibalized the networks' market share. Twenty-four hour news stations have marginalized the networks' national and local news broadcasts. DVRs allow viewers to skip commercials, forcing advertisers to imbed their advertisements in the show through product placements. Now that the FinSyn Rules have been abolished by Congress, the television networks are developing their own programs in-house.

In addition to in-house development, they are demanding a share of ownership of the programs developed by private development companies. Ownership of the programming allows the network to benefit when the show is sold in syndication.

Reality-based programs and talk shows are relatively inexpensive for the networks to produce. As long as the public watches these programs, the networks will show them. Reality stars need representation as they seek to become celebrities and exploit their fifteen minutes of fame. As the industry consolidates and the major studios purchase or create their own networks, the alliances of the independent program producers may change. Also, networks are licensing more movies for television broadcast. Interactive and 3-D television are changing the way consumers view TV.

Movies now typically receive more box office income from foreign exploitation than from their North American release. Catering to foreign markets affects cast choices and storylines. Home video is being replaced by movies on-demand. Developing movies for 3-D theaters and televisions add costs to film budgets.

Video games, YouTube, and Facebook are replacing movies and television viewing for a generation. "The next big thing" will undoubtedly affect the way we create and enjoy media. Entertainment lawyers must keep up with technology to remain relevant. Every new invention creates new challenges for the creative communities as they strive to maintain profits while they protect their intellectual property.

The consensus of opinion concerning opportunities in the entertainment industry is that the supply of interested and qualified lawyers far exceeds the demand. Because many perceive entertainment law practice as being sexy and exciting, students and lawyers both want to get in on the action. While there are some additional benefits, the majority of the work is as exciting or mundane (depending on your point of view) as any other specialty law practice that involves long hours and hard work. When openings due to normal attrition occur, the relatively few new openings go to the most qualified applicants with connections.

EFFECTS OF INDUSTRY GROWTH

Industry growth has been slowed by improvements in corporate fiscal responsibility. As companies continue to merge, there will be fewer opportunities for lawyers on the corporate side of the business. The creative community will continue to create content and find new ways to distribute it to the masses. That creative content will need protection so the creators can benefit from the distribution of their material, and lawyers will be needed to provide that protection for the creative community.

Growth prospects for the industry appear to be steady and cautious. The industry probably will not experience the tremendous growth enjoyed in the late 1960s through the early 1980s. There always will be new talent and new productions, but it will not be the type of reckless expansion previously experienced. Corporate mergers have made the big companies bigger, making it more difficult for independent companies to compete for talent and distribute their products. Most of the major independent companies are purchased by the large multimedia companies as they attempt to gain market share and add to their pool of creative talent. These corporate mergers reduce the number of administrative positions and in-house legal positions available.

TRACKING INDUSTRY TRENDS

New technology has spurred the growth of the entertainment industry growth since it began. The future should be no different. Technological advances in digital audio and video, laser technology, and satellite sophistication all will have an impact on industry growth.

Cable television has already had an impact on the television syndication market and movie licensing. The music industry has changed radically since MTV, the music television network, first came on the air. (There was a time when MTV actually played music videos.) There is a music channel for every popular style of music. Superstations have expanded the impact of regional television stations to a national level. Technology should continue to lead the way in industry expansion.

Entertainment practices must evolve to meet the needs of clients who develop new technology. Technological development is creating novel practice sub-groups in intellectual property and providing new opportunities for qualified lawyers.

Also, as corporations within the new industry areas grow, more may open in-house law departments. International licensing will continue to be a major revenue source for companies, and that will continue to create more opportunities. International political affairs have a tremendous impact on additional markets for all forms of media.

As always, new talent will need representation. However, even though developing talent needs legal advice, the talent may be unable to afford escalating legal fees. Creative billing, or a contingency fee plan, may allow a lawyer to take a risk on new talent and benefit as the talent establishes himself or herself in the industry.

Entrepreneurial productions will create the need for lawyers interested in sharing some of the production cost risks as well as for traditional lawyers who charge an hourly rate. Talented lawyers will find ways to evolve a specialty practice into an entertainment practice if that is a long-term goal.

There will be opportunities, in both corporate and private practice, for lawyers interested in industry-related work. For the foreseeable future, however, the opportunities will be far outnumbered by the number of available qualified lawyers who want to work in the entertainment industry.

Chapter 15

The practice of entertainment law is similar to any other specialty practice where specific substantive expertise is required. A successful private practice requires long hours of work. Each sub-specialty has its own unique problems and legal issues that require an understanding of the business aspects of the industry in addition to the legal specialties. A bibliography of books discussing business aspects of the industry is found in Appendix E. Informed representation requires a background in the business side of the industry, including current trends. Trade publications should be reviewed regularly. Educating yourself on the business of the industry should be part of preparing for a career in entertainment law.

Continuing legal education seminars and symposia on current industry topics are excellent sources of information on both legal issues and business trends. These sessions also may be fruitful sources of contacts. As mentioned previously, having the right connections can help create the break necessary to gain entry into the field. After the initial break, a lawyer is evaluated on the quality of his or her work.

Success in any field requires determination and hard work. Perseverance is necessary to maintain the desire to practice entertainment law while you master a related specialty and develop entertainment clients. Very few recent law school graduates are given the opportunity to begin in an entertainment specialty practice as a first-year associate.

Evaluate your motivation before you dedicate yourself to a career in entertainment law. If you only want to hob-knob with the famous, you will not last long in the industry. Entertainment clients do not want their lawyers to be their best friends. While friendships do develop, they develop out of a professional respect for quality work rather than out of the lawyer's need for a famous playmate.

If your motivation is to work in an exciting industry while using your specialty background to assist clients in their complex legal relationships, then pursue a career as an entertainment lawyer. A good lawyer is a good lawyer in any specialty pursuit. Having an industry reputation for quality representation is the fastest way to expand an entertainment practice, and quality work in a specialty for entertainment clients or their associates can evolve a specialty practice into an entertainment practice.

The practice of entertainment law as a specialty is challenging and exciting. Each client has special needs that create new challenges for the practitioner.

Technological advances also impact the practice of law as new media are developed and exploited, altering the relationships of contractually bound parties. Old contracts must be interpreted to fit new forms of technological exploitation never dreamed of when they were created. Similar issues will continue in the industry.

In addition to a career in private practice there are opportunities as in-house counsel, guild or union practice situations, or in a non-legal career. These positions require expertise in a related field, which can be integrated to meet the needs of the entity, and they are excellent opportunities for lawyers seeking an entry into the industry.

Careers in the entertainment industry not requiring a law degree, such as those discussed in Chapter 9, require an understanding of the business aspects of the industry as well as good interpersonal skills. Being able to work with people is often more important than knowledge of the law for these non-legal positions. However, legal training will help you deal with the industry lawyers on an equal basis, and in turn, this will be a benefit to your clients, and it may attract additional clients. If you are sincerely interested in specializing in entertainment law, you should plot a realistic career path and pursue it. While there is little demand for entertainment lawyers fresh out of law school, there is always a demand for good entertainment lawyers. You can make your own first break by diligently developing a specialty practice.

Earning a place in the industry is a rewarding experience. The financial rewards derived from a good practice can exceed the income derived from a practice in other areas of law. A practice based on quality representation will last for as long as you do. Set realistic practice goals and you can evolve your practice as you gain experience. An entertainment practice takes time and experience to develop, but those who have the perseverance to pursue it will achieve their goals.

Good luck.

Appendix A
GLOSSARY OF INDUSTRY TERMS

The following terms can be helpful in understanding the business of entertainment. They include common slang and industry words of art. Many technical words of art have not been included.

above the line   the portion of a film budget that covers the creative talent associated with the film. Story development costs; script fees; and expenses for actors, the director, producers, and writers

Academy of Motion Picture Arts and Science   (The Academy or AMPAS) the group that presents the Academy Awards show where Oscars are awarded to the winners in various film categories by a vote of the members

acquisition   literary material acquired for exploitation as a television program or movie

A.D.   (Assistant Director) part of the team of directors responsible for helping set up shots, and organizing and coordinating extras, among other things

ADR   (additional dialog recording) recording done in a studio by an actor to fix mistakes in the dialog track of the film; see also *looping*

advance   money paid to talent as an upfront fee that is typically recoupable from royalties.   In music, recording expenses can be included in the advance. Advances are generally non-recoupable.

agent   an individual who solicits, on behalf of his or her client, employment in the industry or the rights to material. Guilds and unions regulate agents who represent their members. In addition, some states regulate the conduct of agents in their jurisdiction.

airplay   refers to whether and for how long a song is played on the radio

Alan Smithee   (also Allen Smithee) prior to the 1997 film *An Alan Smithee Film: Burn Hollywood Burn* the pseudonym authorized by the Directors Guild of America (DGA) for use by a director who no longer wished to be affiliated with the film. After the film, the DGA allows directors to use a project specific pseudonym if the director feels that the film has been edited in a way that no longer represents the director's vision.

American Federation of Television and Radio Artists   (AFTRA) the guild that represents television and radio talent

American Society of Cinematographers   (ASC) an invitation-only membership group dedicated to advancing the art of cinematography

arthouse   a motion picture exhibition house that shows foreign and independent films

A&R   (artist and repertoire) the record company department in charge of finding and signing new artists. A&R people act as the liaison between the record company and the talent.

Association of Motion Picture and Television Producers   (AMPTP) a trade organization for content producers

ASCAP   (American Society of Composers, Authors and Publishers) see *performing rights organization*

atmosphere   a term for background actors or extras

auteur theory   a French theory that posits that the director is the true creator (auteur) of a film because he or she provides the creative vision to produce the art that is the finished film

back end   the profit participation in the gross or net proceeds of a film

background actor   an extra or atmosphere actor

backlot   the undeveloped area at a studio where wilderness scenes can be filmed and open air sets can be constructed

below the line   the portion of the budget that includes all of the physical production costs not included in the above-the-line portion of the budget. Expenses for camera equipment, catering, crew, film stock, music, publicity (prints and advertisements), trailers, and any other expense that does not belong in the above-the-line budget.

best boy   an assistant. For example the best boy grip is the key grip's assistant, and the best boy electric is the key gaffer's assistant

blocking   rehearsal movements designed to allow the actors and the director to visualize the scene and movement prior to filming the scene

BMI   (Broadcast Music, Inc.) see *performing rights organization*

bootleg   unauthorized copy of a copyrighted work, such as a unauthorized recording, including a recording of a live performance. Bootleg copies are made for distribution.

business manager   a person who manages money for industry people who are too busy or make too much money to manage their own; the chief administrator and negotiator for a union or guild

buyout   a onetime payment for the use of a performance or intellectual property that relieves the purchaser from the duty to pay royalties

callback   a second audition

call sheet   the daily shooting schedule listing the actors necessary for the each scene, including each actor's reporting time, the scenes to be shot, and the crews' arrival times

choreographer   the person who creates and directs the dance sequences in a production

clearance   the act of securing the rights to intellectual property for use in a production or song

clout   the power, connections, and ability to make deals happen

commercial   having mass public appeal. Examples include a blockbuster movie, a popular television show, and a song with a saleable sound.

composer   the person who writes the music in a musical composition

compulsory license   a licensed that allows a third party to make a sound recording of a copyright owner's musical composition without the copyright owner's permission

Coogan's law   a group of laws that govern the employment of children in the entertainment industry named after Jackie Coogan, a child actor who was exploited by his parents and advisors

cover record   the recording of a sound recording by someone who did not write the musical composition. The performer can negotiate a license to "cover" the musical composition, or the performer can obtain a compulsory license and record the song without the copyright owner's permission

coverage   a brief summary of a script or book prepared by readers and creative executives as a reference so that the decision maker can discuss the script as if he or she read it. Coverage usually includes an evaluation of the idea, the script, and the writer.

"created by"   the credit given to the writer of the pilot episode of a television show

credits   (also, screen credits) name recognition printed at the beginning or end of a television program or a movie, on the record jacket of an album, or in a theatrical program or playbill

cross collateralization   the contractual technique of tying the expenses and income of one product (song, album, film, etc.) to the expenses and income of the other products in the cross-collateralization pool

dailies   the film shot on a single day of a feature film. The producer, director, and studio executive watch dailies to make sure they are getting the shots they need for a film.

development   the preproduction process where the script is rewritten in anticipation of production

Director's Guild of America   (DGA) the collective bargaining organization for directors

dramaturg   an individual who researches and interprets all aspects of a play for the actors and director to ensure authenticity in the production. The Dramaturg typically will write program notes for the Playbill.

establishing shot   an introductory shot used to establish the location and setting of the upcoming scene

extras   performers who generally do not recite lines in a production

first dollar gross   the most preferred back-end participation situation where the recipient receives a percentage of the gross income of the film. Gross income, for purposes of this calculation, includes all income minus deductions for taxes and trade association dues.

four-walling   the act of renting a venue for a flat fee. In this situation, the event producer pays for all of the production expenses and keeps all of the revenue generated by the event. The venue is not entitled to a percentage of the box office receipts.

gaffer the head of the electrical department and the person in charge of the grips.

gig a job

gold record the award presented for album or singles sales in excess of 500,000

green light the term used to indicate that a project is approved for production

grip a person who works with the lighting and electrical equipment on the set

guild the collective bargaining unit engaged in the representation of talent

hiatus the off-season for production of a television series when the cast and crew are free to work on other projects or enjoy a vacation

high concept the term used to describe a movie that includes elements designed to appeal to the largest possible audience

hook the musical phrase or chorus that catches the ear in a song. A good hook will have the listener singing along after the first play of the song.

hype sensational publicity to stimulate interest in a media project

image the public's impression of an artist, group, or production

International Alliance of Theatrical Stage Employees, Moving Picture Technicians, Artists and Allied Crafts (IATSE) a collective bargaining organization for people named in the title

key gaffer the person who is in charge of scheduling the people and equipment necessary for each day of filming

key grip the lead grip in charge of camera movement and lighting

lead sheet sheet music that includes the lyrics and the melody of a song

legitimate stage rights the right to present literary material before a live audience

literary agent   a person who represents script writers in both film and television

line producer   the producer responsible for the details of the daily production and who is responsible for keeping the production on time and on budget

log line   a one-sentence summary of the idea or plot of a story. The log line is always included in a pitch.

looping   the matching of dialog to lip movement on the screen; see also *ADR*

lyricist   the person who writes the words to a musical composition

MacGuffin   (also Mcguffin) the desired object of the film character's pursuit. Alfred Hitchcock used the term to describe the "thing" that the characters must have in order to solve the mystery or save the day.

mail room   the place where an agent trainee program begins. Trainees learn the office personnel by delivering the mail. Agent trainees who hope to move on, read scripts at night and prepare coverage of the scripts for the agents.

manager   the person who guides an artist's career

mechanical royalties   (mechanicals) song royalties paid based on the number of records sold. Mechanical rights are obtained by a record company from a music publishing company, which collects the royalties from the record company and pays the songwriters a negotiated percentage

merchandising   the licensing, manufacture, distribution, and sale of merchandise based on or connected with a group, artist, character, or production

mogul   a person who has earned industry recognition and clout

monkey points   see *net profit*

music publisher   the individual or company that exploits musical compositions, collects and distributes royalties, and protects the copyrights on behalf of songwriters

negative costs the actual cost of a finished film, which may include overhead expenses and the cost of the money spent on the production

negative pickup the purchase of a completed film by a distributor

net profit the amount of money earned by a project after all of the expenses have been deducted. Eddie Murphy referred to net profits as monkey points because there is almost never any money left for distribution of net profits after all of the deductions have been taken

network television broadcast nationally. According to Federal Communications Commission (FCC) regulations, a network must provide a *minimum* of fifteen hours of programming per week and must have a minimum of twenty-five affiliated licensees in ten or more states.

one sheet a one-page advertisement for a film or television show used in newspapers, magazines, and on billboards and bus stops, wherever the film is advertised. It normally includes credits.

P&A prints and advertisements for publicizing a movie

payola money paid by record companies and record promoters to radio stations to encourage the station to play a particular song. Payola has been outlawed by Congress.

performing rights organization an organizations that collect performance royalties from radio stations, television stations, and internet broadcasters on behalf of music publishing companies and songwriters. ASCAP (American Society of Composers, Authors and Publishers), BMI (Broadcast Music, Inc.), and SESAC (Society of European Stage Authors and Composers) are the three major performing rights societies in the United States.

production assistant (PA) an entry-level position in a film production. PAs usually perform menial tasks for the above-the-line participants.

performance rights the right to publicly perform the music and lyrics of a musical composition

pitch   an oral summary of a story idea usually delivered by a producer or a writer to a creative executive

platinum record   the award for album and single sales in excess of one million

playbill   the program for a live theatrical performance that includes the biographies of the producers, director, writer, and actors. It usually includes the dramaturg's notes and other information about the production.

playwright   the writer of the script for a live theatrical performance. The playwright participates in the casting and rehearsals for the play and must approve any changes in the script.

points   a percentage of the income or profits from a project. The definition of points in a contract is sometimes the most complicated section of the contract requiring intense negotiation by both parties. The definition varies depending on the amount of clout the individual seeking the points has. Both gross points and net points are negotiated as part of an individual's compensation package.

producer   the person responsible for the overall business and creative production of a project. The producer is like the chief executive officer of a small company. The producer and his or her production company employ all of the people who work on a project.

Producers Guild of America   (PGA) the collective bargaining organization for producers

program director   the radio station employee who decides which songs the station will play and how often they will be played. The program director was usually the recipient of secret payola.

project hell   see *turnaround*

public domain   material that is not protected by copyrights, patents, or trademarks. Public domain material may be used by anyone without payment for the underlying rights.

recoupment   the accounting process whereby all costs of production are recovered from the receipts created by exploitation (sales) of the product.

residuals   fees paid to actors for the repeated use of material. Residuals are usually negotiated by the various guilds.

royalties   money payable to performers based on the exploitation (sales) of the intellectual property. Musical performers receive royalties for record sales and from digital public performances. Songwriters and music publishing companies receive royalties from song sales and public performances.

scale   the minimum wage to be paid to a person who is a member of a guild or union

score   the musical compositions which make up the soundtrack of a production.

Screen Actor's Guild   (SAG) the collective bargaining organization for screen actors

Screen Extra's Guild   (SEG) the collective bargaining organization for screen extras

SESAC   (Society of European Stage Authors and Composers) see *performing rights organization*

set dressing   items placed around the set to complement the scene and make the set appear more authentic

sound track   the dialogue, music, and sound effects that accompany the pictures in a visual production

spec script   a non-commissioned script written with the hope that a studio will purchase it for production

superstation   a television station that broadcasts by satellite to geographic areas outside the local territory (usually over cable television)

synchronization rights   the rights required to use a musical composition in an audiovisual work. Typically, a music publishing company will issue a synchronization license to a production company for the use of the musical composition in a film or television show.

Taft-Hartley Act   the law that allows a non-union actor to work on a union film as long as it is the actor's first film.

talent   the term for the creative people who write, direct, perform, and produce the industry's products

trades   regular publications with entertainment news, including *Variety, The Hollywood Reporter, Billboard,* and the "Company Town" section in the *Los Angeles Times.* Industry professionals read these and other publications regularly to keep up to date.

Treatment   a synopsis of a work prepared by a writer that shows the plot, setting, and development of characters. A treatment is usually written to give the creative executives an idea of the writer's interpretation of the show. Treatments can also be created from a finished work. The treatment for a television show includes future story ideas and character development.

turnaround   (project hell) the state of limbo created when a project is dropped by a studio. The producers generally have the right to find a new studio for the production, but the new studio must pay the previous studio for its costs incurred before the project was placed in turnaround.

Unit Production Manager   (UPM)

wide release   the initial release of a film across the nation in on as many screens as economically feasible. Generally, a wide release will be an opening on one thousand or more screens.

There are numerous websites and publications that list and explain industry terms:

- www.actorschecklist.com/resources/glossary.html

- www.hollyword.org

- www.imdb.com/glossary

- www.marklitwak.com/glossary-of-industry-terms.html

- www.sfcv.org/learn/glossary?gclid=C

- www.variety.com/static-pages/slanguage-dictionary/

Appendix B
INDUSTRY ORGANIZATIONS

The following are industry organizations serving talent members specializing in the field.

Academy of Country Music
www.acmcountry.com
5500 Balboa Boulevard
Encino, CA 91316
(818) 788-8000 (p)
(818) 788-0999 (f)

Academy of Motion Picture Arts and Sciences
www.oscars.org
8949 Wilshire Boulevard
Beverly Hills, CA 90211
(310) 247-3000

Academy of Television Arts and Sciences
www.emmys.com
www.emmys.tv/
5220 Lankershim Boulevard
North Hollywood, CA 91601
(818) 754-2800

Actor's Equity
www.actorsequity.org

Western Region
6755 Hollywood Boulevard, 5th Floor
Hollywood, CA 90028
(323) 978-8080 (p)
(323) 978-8081 (f)

Central Region
Actors' Equity Building
557 West Randolph Street
Chicago, IL 60661
(312) 641-0393 (p)
(312) 641-6365 (f)

Eastern Region
165 West 46th Street
New York, NY 10036
(212) 869-8530 (p)
(212) 719-9015 (f)

Orlando Sattelite Office
10319 Orangewood Boulevard
Orlando, FL 32821
(407) 345-8600 (p)
(407) 345-1522 (f)

American Cinema Editors
www.ace-filmeditors.org
100 Universal City Plaza
Verna Fields Building 2282, Room 190
Universal City, CA 91608
(818) 772-2900 (p)
(818) 733-5023 (f)

American Film Institute
www.afi.com
2021 North Western Avenue
Hollywood, CA 90027
(213) 856-7600 (p)
(323) 467-4578 (f)

American Film Market
www.americanfilmmarket.com
10850 Wilshire Boulevard, 9th Floor
Los Angeles, CA 90024-4321
(310) 446-1000 (p)
(310) 446-1600 (f)

American Guild of Musical Artists
www.musicalartists.org
1430 Broadway
New York, NY 10018
(212) 265-3687 (p)
(212) 262-9088

American Guild of Variety Artists (AGVA)
www.agvausa.com

National Office
363 Seventh Avenue, 17th Floor
New York, NY 10001-3904
(212) 675-1003 (p)
(212) 633-0097 (f)

West Coast Office
11712 Moorpark Street, Suite 110
Studio City, CA 91604
(818) 508-9984 (p)
(818) 508-3029 (f)

American Society of Cinematographers

www.theasc.com

1782 North Orange Drive

Hollywood, CA 90028

(800) 448-0145 (p)

(323) 882-6391 (f)

American Society of Composers, Authors and Publishers (ASCAP)

www.ascap.com

ASCAP — New York

1900 Broadway

New York, NY 10023

(212) 621-6000 (p)

(212) 621-8453 (f)

ASCAP — London

8 Cork Street

London W1S3LJ

011-44-207-439-0909 (p)

011-44-207-434-0073 (f)

ASCAP — Miami

420 Lincoln Rd, Suite 385

Miami Beach, FL 33139

(305) 673-3446 (p)

(305) 673-2446 (f)

ASCAP — Puerto Rico

Ave. Martinez Nadal

c/ Hill Side 623

San Juan, PR 00920

(787) 707-0782 (p)

(787) 707-0783 (f)

ASCAP — Los Angeles
7920 West Sunset Boulevard,
Third Floor
Los Angeles, CA 90046
(323) 883-1000 (p)
(323) 883-1049 (f)

ASCAP — Nashville
Two Music Square West
Nashville, TN 37203
(615) 742-5000 (p)
(615) 742-5020 (f)

ASCAP — Atlanta
950 Joseph E. Lowery Blvd. NW, Suite 23
Atlanta, GA 30318
(404) 685-8699 (p)
(404) 685-8701 (f)

Association of Talent Agents (ATA)
www.agentassociation.com
9255 Sunset Boulevard, Suite 930
Los Angeles, CA 90069
(310) 274-0628 (p)
(310) 274-5063 (f)

Black Stuntmen's Association
www.blackstuntmensassociation.com
Las Vegas, NV
(702) 646-3626

Casting Society of America
www.castingsociety.com
606 North Larchmont Boulevard, Suite 4-B
Los Angeles, CA 90004-1309
(323) 463-1925 (p)

National Conference of Personal Managers

www.ncopm.com

10231 Riverside Drive

North Hollywood, CA 91602-2500

(866) 916-2676 (P)

Country Music Association

www.cmaworld.com

1 Music Circle South

Nashville, TN 37203

(615) 244-2840?

Director's Guild of America (DGA)

www.dga.org

National Headquarters

7920 West Sunset Boulevard

Los Angeles, CA 90046

(310) 289-2000 (p)

(800) 421-4173 (p)

New York

110 West 57th Street

New York, NY 10019

(212) 258-0800 (p)

(800) 356-3754 (p)

Chicago

400 North Michigan Avenue, Suite 307

Chicago, Il 60611

(312) 644-5050 (p)

(888) 660-6975 (p)

Dramatist Guild
www.dramatistsguild.com
1501 Broadway, Suite 701
New York, NY 10036
(212) 398-9366 (p)
(212) 944-0420 (f)

Entertainment Law Committee
Beverly Hills Bar Association
www.bhba.org
9420 Wilshire Boulevard, 2nd Floor
Beverly Hills, CA 90212-3169
(310) 610-2422 (p)
(310) 601-2423 (f)

Film Advisory Board, Inc.
www.filmadvisoryboard.com
c/o Janet Stokes
263 West Olive Avenue, #377
Burbank, CA 91502
(323) 461-6541 (p)
(323) 469-8541 (f)

International Alliance of Theatrical Stage Employees (IATSE)
www.iatse-intl.org

General Office
207 West 25th Street, 4th Floor
New York, NY 10001
(212) 730-1770 (p)
(212) 730-7809 (f)

West Coast Office
10045 Riverside Drive
Toluca Lake, CA 91602
(818) 980-3499 (p)
(818) 980-3496 (f)

International Documentary Association
www.documentary.org
3470 Wilshire Boulevard, Suite 980
Los Angeles, CA 90010
(213) 232-1660 (p)
(213) 232-1669 (f)

International Stunt Association
www.isastunts.com
(818) 501-5225 (p)
(818) 501-5656 (f)

Motion Picture Association of America (MPAA)
www.mpaa.org

Washington, D.C.
1600 Eye St., NW
Washington, D.C. 20006
(202) 293-1966 (p)
(202) 296-7410 (f)

Los Angeles
15301 Ventura Blvd., Building E
Sherman Oaks, CA 91403
(818) 995-6600 (p)
(818) 285-4403 (f)

New York
500 Mamaroneck Ave , Suite 403
Harrison NY 10528
(914) 333-8892 (p)
(914) 333-7541 (f)

Dallas
1425 Greenway Dr., Suite 270
Irving, TX 75038
(972) 756-9078 (p)
(972) 756-9402 (f)

Sao Paulo, Brazil
Rua Jerônimo da Veiga, 45, Conj 121/122, 12º Floor
Jardim Europa, São Paulo, S.P
04536-000, Brazil
011-55-11-3667-2080 (p)
www.mpaal.org.br

Brussels, Belgium
Motion Picture Association
Brussels office
Avenue des Arts 46 box 8
B — 1000 Brussels
+32 2 778 27 11 (p)
+32 2 778 27 00 or +32 2 778 27 50 (f)

Mexico City, Mexico
Lafontaine #42
Chapultepec Polanco
Mexico, 11560 DF
011-5255 5280 6878/5281 6090 (p)

Singapore
#04-07 Central Mall
No. 1 Magazine Road
Singapore 059567
+65 6253 1033 (p)
+65 6255 1838 (f)
www.mpa-i.org/

Toronto, Canada
55 St. Clair Avenue, West, Suite 210
Toronto, ON M4V 2Y7
(416) 961-1888 (p)
(416) 968-1016 (f)
www.mpa-canada.org

Nashville Musicians Association
www.nashvillemusicians.org
11 Music Circle North
P. O. Box 120399
Nashville, TN 37212
(615) 244-9514 (p)
(615) 259-9140 (f)

National Academy of Recording Arts and Sciences (NARAS)
www.grammy.com
3030 Olympic Boulevard
Santa Monica, CA 90404
(310) 392-3777 (p)
(310) 399-3090 (f)

National Association of Broadcast Employees
and Technicians (NABET)
www.nabetcwa.org
501 3rd Street NW
Washington, D.C. 20001
(202) 434-1254 (p)
(202) 434-1426 (f)

National Academy of Television Arts and Sciences
www.emmyonline.com
1697 Broadway, Suite 404
New York, NY 10019
(212) 586-8424 (p)
(212) 246-8129 (f)

Producer's Guild of America, Inc.
www.producersguild.org
8530 Wilshire Boulevard, Suite 400
Beverly Hills, CA 90211

   PGA East
   100 Avenue of the Americas, Suite 1240
   New York, NY 10013

Screen Actor's Guild (SAG)
www.sagaftra.org

National Headquarters
5757 Wilshire Boulevard, 7th Floor
Los Angeles, CA 90036-3635
(323) 954-1600 (SAG)
(323) 634-8100 (AFTRA)

New York Office
360 Madison Avenue, 12th Floor
New York, NY 10016
(212) 532-0800 (p)

Songwriters Guild of America
www.songwritersguild.com
5120 Virginia Way, Suite C22
Brentwood, TN 37027
(615) 742-9945 (p)
(800) 524-6742 (p)
(615) 630-7501 (f)

Stuntmen's Association of Motion Pictures, Inc.
www.stuntmen.com
5200 Lankershim Boulevard, Suite 190
North Hollywood, CA 91601
(818) 766-4334 (p)
(818) 766-5943 (f)

Stuntwomen's Association of Motion Pictures
www.stuntwomen.com
3760 Cahuenga Boulevard, Suite 104
Studio City, CA 91644
(818) 588-8888 (p)
(818) 762-0907 (f)

Women In Film
http://www.wif.org
6100 Wilshire Boulevard, Suite 710
Los Angeles, CA 90048
(323) 935-2211 (p)
(323) 935-2212 (f)

Women in Music
www.womeninmusic.org

Writer's Guild of America, West, Inc.
www.wga.org
7000 West Third Street
Los Angeles, CA 90048
(323) 951-4000 (p)
(800) 548-4532 (p)
(323) 782-4800 (f)

Writer's Guild of America, East, Inc.
www.wgaeast.org
250 Hudson Street, Suite 700
New York, NY 10013
(212) 767-7800 (p)
(212) 582-1909 (f)

Appendix C
TRADE PUBLICATIONS

The following publications are commonly read industry reporters.

Billboard Magazine
www.billboard.com

Cashbox Magazine
www.cashboxmagazine.com

Filmbiz
http://www.filmbiz.com/entertainment-industry/entertainment-industry-business/Trade_
Publications.php

Hollywood Reporter
www.hollywoodreporter.com

Pollstar USA
www.pollstar.com

Variety
www.variety.com

Appendix D

GENERAL CAREER PLANNING GUIDE

The following websites and publications are general career planning guides which should prove helpful in evaluating your career and planning your next career move.

http://www.americanbar.org/resources_for_lawyers/careercenter.html
http://www.usajobs.gov/
http://www.lawfirmjobsearch.com
http://careers.findlaw.com
http://jobline.acc.com
http://www.martindale.com/Careers/Careers.aspx
http://www.legalcareernetwork.com
http://hound.com

For an extensive list of career planning publications, use the search term *career planning* or *career planning books* at:
http://www.barnesandnoble.com
or
http://www.amazon.com

Appendix E

The following publications and websites offer information on jobs and the business aspects of the entertainment industry.

http://www.americanbar.org/resources_for_lawyers/careercenter/entertainment_sports_law_jobs.html
http://www.entertainmentcareers.net/jcat.asp?jcat=117
http://www.showbizjobs.com/dsp_jobsearch.cfm
http://www.careerbuilder.com/Jobs/Keyword/Entertaiment-Lawyer/
http://www.indeed.com/q-Entertainment-Law-jobs.html
http://www.simplyhired.com/k-entertainment-law-jobs.html

For an up-to-date list of books available, use the search term *entertainment* or *entertainment books* at one of these sites:
http://www.barnesandnoble.com
http://www.amazon.com

Index

How to Start and Build a Law Practice, 5th Ed
By Jay G. Foonberg

Product Code: 5110508 • LP Price: $57.95 • Regular Price: $69.95

If you have a question about starting and growing your own law practice, or improving your existing solo or small firm practice, Jay Foonberg has the answers in this power-packed, updated, and expanded new edition. Learn it all from a practicing lawyer who provides you with real answers, for real practices, gained from real experiences.

This classic ABA bestseller has been used by tens of thousands of lawyers as the comprehensive guide to planning, launching, and growing a successful practice. It's packed with over 600 pages of guidance on identifying the right location, finding clients, setting fees, managing your office, maintaining an ethical and responsible practice, maximizing available resources, upholding your standards, and much more. If you're committed to starting your own practice, this book will give you the expert advice you need to make it succeed.

The Lawyer's Essential Guide to Writing
By Marie Buckley

Product Code: 5110726 • LP Price: $47.95 • Regular Price: $79.95

This is a readable, concrete guide to contemporary legal writing. Based on Marie Buckley's years of experience coaching lawyers, this book provides a systematic approach to all forms of written communication, from memoranda and briefs to e-mail and blogs. The book sets forth three principles for powerful writing and shows how to apply those principles to develop a clean and confident style.

LinkedIn in One Hour for Lawyers, 2nd Ed.
By Dennis Kennedy and Allison C. Shields

Product Code: 5110773 • LP Price: $39.95 • Regular Price: $49.95

Since the first edition of LinkedIn in One Hour for Lawyers was published, LinkedIn has added almost 100 million users, and more and more lawyers are using the platform on a regular basis. Now, this bestselling ABA book has been fully revised and updated to reflect significant changes to LinkedIn's layout and functionality made through 2013. LinkedIn in One Hour for Lawyers, Second Edition, will help lawyers make the most of their online professional networking. In just one hour, you will learn to:

- Set up a LinkedIn® account
- Create a robust, dynamic profile--and take advantage of new multimedia options
- Build your connections
- Enhance your Company Page with new functionality
- Use search tools to enhance your network
- Monitor your network with ease
- Optimize your settings for privacy concerns
- Use LinkedIn® effectively in the hiring process
- Develop a LinkedIn strategy to grow your legal network

The Legal Career Guide, 5th Edition
By Gary A. Munneke, Ellen Wayne

Product Code: 5110667 • LP Price: $34.95 • Regular Price: $54.95

With a few simple steps, lawyers can use Facebook® to market their services, grow their practices, and expand their legal network—all by using the same methods they already use to communicate with friends and family. *Facebook® in One Hour for Lawyers* will show any attorney—from Facebook® novices to advanced users—how to use this powerful tool for both professional and personal purposes.

Job Quest for Lawyers: The Essential Guide to Finding and Landing the Job You Want
By Sheila Nielsen

Product Code: 5110725 • LP Price: $39.95 • Regular Price: $49.95

Job Quest for Lawyers provides step-by-step guidance that finally makes networking inspiring instead of a chore. The "quest" motif applies to each stage of the job search, and is used to help readers understand how to create a positive and effective networking experience. The book demystifies networking by including illustrations from the author's own experiences and from the stories of her clients that provide examples of the real world do's and don'ts of how to conduct a productive job search. Unlike so many other career books, Job Quest for Lawyers is a process-focused book that is eminently applicable to attorneys at all phases of their careers, from new graduates to senior lawyers. Lawyers at all stages of practice will benefit from reading this book.

Entertainment Careers for Lawyers, 3rd Ed.
By William D. Henslee

Product Code: 5110769 • LP Price: $32.95 • Regular Price: $54.95

Entertainment Careers for Lawyers, Third Edition, will dispel many of the myths surrounding the practice and help lawyers and law students gain an understanding of the realities of entertainment law. Written by William D. Henslee, an experienced entertainment lawyer and law professor, this book will help you gain an overview of the substantive law areas included in entertainment law, from intellectual property and litigation to contract negotiations and estate planning. You will also earn about the career trajectories available in four major entertainment genres: music, theater, film, and television.

Nonlegal Careers for Lawyers, Fifth Edition
By William D. Henslee, Gary A. Munneke, Ellen Wayne

Product Code: 5110567 • LP Price: $29.95 • Regular Price: $34.95

Perhaps you are a law student who realizes that practicing law is not what you want to do. Or maybe you are a practicing lawyer who no longer feels satisfied with your work. If you feel it's time for a change, this newly revised guidebook will show you what you can do with your law degree, besides practice law. More importantly, this book will illustrate how to use your legal skills to rise above the competition.

iPad in One Hour for Lawyers, Second Edition
By Tom Mighell

Product Code: 5110747 • LP Price: $24.95 • Regular Price: $39.95

Whether you are a new or a more advanced iPad user, *iPad in One Hour for Lawyers* takes a great deal of the mystery and confusion out of using your iPad. Ideal for lawyers who want to get up to speed swiftly, this book presents the essentials so you don't get bogged down in technical jargon and extraneous features and apps. In just six, short lessons, you'll learn how to:

- Quickly Navigate and Use the iPad User Interface
- Set Up Mail, Calendar, and Contacts
- Create and Use Folders to Multitask and Manage Apps
- Add Files to Your iPad, and Sync Them
- View and Manage Pleadings, Case Law, Contracts, and other Legal Documents
- Use Your iPad to Take Notes and Create Documents
- Use Legal-Specific Apps at Trial or in Doing Research

Personal Branding In One Hour for Lawyers
By Katy Goshtasbi

Product Code: 5110765 • LP Price: $39.95 • Regular Price: $49.95

With over 1.2 million licensed attorneys in the United States, how do lawyers stand out from their fellow practitioners and get jobs, promotions, clients, and referrals? To survive and thrive, lawyers must develop their own intentional personal brand to distinguish themselves from the competition. In Personal Branding in One Hour for Lawyers, personal branding expert and experienced attorney Katy Goshtasbi explains how attorneys can highlight their unique talents and abilities, manage their perceptions, and achieve greater success as a lawyer in the process. In just one hour, you will learn to:

- Discover your personal brand--and why it matters to colleagues and clients
- Use your personal brand as a marketing tool
- Stand out from the crowd--improve your visual brand by making simple, yet impactful, changes to your attire and personal appearance
- Create effective marketing materials for your brand
- Network successfully to implement your personal brand
- Communicate your brand effectively

The Lawyer's Guide to Professional Coaching
By Andrew Elowitt

Product Code: 5110735 • LP Price: $47.95 • Regular Price: $79.95

Become more efficient and profitable in your law practice by employing a professional coach. The Lawyer's Guide to Professional Coaching will teach you to find, select, and work productively with the right coach for your needs--and transform your practice in the process. Learn how to get the most out of coaching, decide whether coaching is right for you and your firm, and use coaching skills when you manage, mentor, and collaborate with client and colleagues.

Lessons in Leadership: Essential Skills for Lawyers
By Thomas C. Grella

Product Code: 5110761 • LP Price: $47.95 • Regular Price: $79.95

More lawyers than ever before are using Twitter to network with colleagues, attract clients, market their law firms, and even read the news. But to the uninitiated, Twitter's short messages, or tweets, can seem like they are written in a foreign language. Twitter in One Hour for Lawyers will demystify one of the most important social-media platforms of our time and teach you to tweet like an expert. In just one hour, you will learn to:

- Create a Twitter account and set up your profile
- Read tweets and understand Twitter jargon
- Write tweets—and send them at the appropriate time
- Gain an audience—follow and be followed
- Engage with other Twitters users
- Integrate Twitter into your firm's marketing plan
- Cross-post your tweets with other social media platforms like Facebook and LinkedIn
- Understand the relevant ethics, privacy, and security concerns
- Get the greatest possible return on your Twitter investment

Virtual Law Practice: How to Deliver Legal Services Online
By Stephanie L. Kimbro

Product Code: 5110707 • LP Price: $47.95 • Regular Price: $79.95

The legal market has recently experienced a dramatic shift as lawyers seek out alternative methods of practicing law and providing more affordable legal services. Virtual law practice is revolutionizing the way the public receives legal services and how legal professionals work with clients. If you are interested in this form of practicing law, *Virtual Law Practice* will help you:

- Responsibly deliver legal services online to your clients
- Successfully set up and operate a virtual law office
- Establish a virtual law practice online through a secure, client-specific portal
- Manage and market your virtual law practice
- Understand state ethics and advisory opinions
- Find more flexibility and work/life balance in the legal profession

The Lawyer's Essential Guide to Writing
By Marie Buckley

Product Code: 5110726 • LP Price: $47.95 • Regular Price: $79.95

This is a readable, concrete guide to contemporary legal writing. Based on Marie Buckley's years of experience coaching lawyers, this book provides a systematic approach to all forms of written communication, from memoranda and briefs to e-mail and blogs. The book sets forth three principles for powerful writing and shows how to apply those principles to develop a clean and confident style.

30-DAY RISK-FREE ORDER FORM

ABA LAW PRACTICE DIVISION
The Business of Practicing Law

Please print or type. To ship UPS, we must have your street address. If you list a P.O. Box, we will ship by U.S. Mail.

Name

Member ID

Firm/Organization

Street Address

City/State/Zip

Area Code/Phone (In case we have a question about your order)

E-mail

Method of Payment:
☐ Check enclosed, payable to American Bar Association
☐ MasterCard ☐ Visa ☐ American Express

Card Number   Expiration Date

Signature Required

MAIL THIS FORM TO:
American Bar Association, Publication Orders
P.O. Box 10892, Chicago, IL 60610

ORDER BY PHONE:
24 hours a day, 7 days a week:
Call 1-800-285-2221 to place a credit card order. We accept Visa, MasterCard, and American Express.

EMAIL ORDERS: orders@americanbar.org
FAX ORDERS: 1-312-988-5568

VISIT OUR WEB SITE: www.ShopABA.org
Allow 7-10 days for regular UPS delivery. Need it sooner? Ask about our overnight delivery options. Call the ABA Service Center at 1-800-285-2221 for more information.

GUARANTEE:
If–for any reason–you are not satisfied with your purchase, you may return it within 30 days of receipt for a refund of the price of the book(s). No questions asked.

Thank You For Your Order.

Join the ABA Law Practice Division today and receive a substantial discount on Division publications!

Product Code:	Description:	Quantity:	Price:	Total Price:
				$
				$
				$
				$
				$

Shipping/Handling:		**Tax:**		
$0.00 to $9.99	add $0.00	IL residents add 9.25%	**Subtotal:**	$
$10.00 to $49.99	add $6.95	DC residents add 5.75%	***Tax:**	$
$50.00 to $99.99	add $8.95		****Shipping/Handling:**	$
$100.00 to $199.99	add $10.95	Yes, I am an ABA member and would like to join the Law Practice Division today! (Add $50.00)		$
$200.00 to $499.99	add $13.95		**Total:**	$